# Welcome to 1960s Dutch Harbor, Alaska

## The Cow Woman of Akutan's Life on a Deserted Military Base

BY JOAN BROWN DODD

*PO Box 221974 Anchorage, Alaska 99522-1974*
*books@publicationconsultants.com—www.publicationconsultants.com*

ISBN 978-1-59433-702-4
eBook ISBN 978-1-59433-703-1
Library of Congress Catalog Card Number: 2017937564


—First Edition—



Manufactured in the United States of America.

Author of

*Cow Woman of Akutan*

# Dedication

Becky Leigh Pfeil and
Malcolm Gerard Brown
This is your story too.

# Acknowledgments

*A lot* of people contributed in one way or another to the writing of this story. Some did hands-on editing, while others provided information, read, listened, and/or encouraged me to keep at it. To name a few, my husband Doug, my daughter and son Becky and Malcolm, who were there and jogged my memory more than once, Tina Kudrin Gauen, a true daughter of the Aleutians and good friend, Sharon Svarny-Livingston, daughter of my friend Gert and provider of information as my eighty-three year old memory is sometimes short on details, Piama Oleyer, daughter of Mary Robinson who later went by Maria Turnpaugh, who was helpful in a similar way, including her constant encouragement, my Homer reading group who are responsible for my having to make a few grammar corrections and re-writes, Dr. Michael Livingston, researcher extraordinaire and one of my strongest motivators when I was feeling sort of lazy, with his "Get crackin'!" This is also a good place to thank the many readers of my previous book who have written, called or approached me and not only expressed an interest in that story but wanted to know when I would have another book finished. Well, here it is. Thanks to all of you for your help.

# Contents

1962, Abandoned Military Base, Dutch Harbor.

*Chapter*

# 1

# Welcome to Dutch Harbor

*The small* DC-3 with its handful of passengers wove in and out of blinding snow squalls in the Alaskan winter darkness that late afternoon in April, 1961. Through the open cockpit door I watched wide-eyed as the pilot and co-pilot bounced up and down in their seats to the unrelenting rhythm of the plane. The only break in its otherwise continuous rocking was an occasional abrupt drop, followed by a sharp upward jerk before resuming the bouncing motion. For obvious safety reasons, the severe turbulence prevented the stewardess from leaving her seat for most of that flight to the almost deserted island of Dutch Harbor in the Aleutian Islands. The one hour flight out of Cold Bay, Alaska gave me ample time to reflect on my situation.

Earlier that morning, accompanied by my two children, Malcolm, age one and Becky, four, I had taken the DC-6, a larger plane, out of Anchorage, Alaska to Cold Bay, the last community on the mainland before the Aleutian Chain began. The three hour flight had been uneventful and the children were fairly quiet. Though the plane was smaller than my jet experience, I thought that it wasn't so bad.

After a smooth landing at that tiny community on the tip of the Alaska Peninsula, we changed to the DC-3, the smallest plane I had ever flown in. I felt that maybe I was becoming a pro at air travel, though not necessarily something I wanted to aspire to, certainly not at the moment, not in that weather.

In one short month I had flown in two jets and a DC-6, and now here I was boarding plane number four, a DC-3. I felt a little smug that I was the first in my family to fly in an airplane, though planes had been around for many years. My parents were always a bit skeptical about the latest inventions. For example, we still watched a black-and-white television while our neighbors had color televisions, and we still used a wringer washer after automatic washers were showing up everywhere.

Now I was on my way to the far-flung chain of Aleutian Islands, often referred to simply as the Chain. They dotted the North Pacific in a huge arc, extending for many hundreds of miles. On the map the tip of the Chain looked awfully close to an imaginary line separating the US from Russia. Of the islands that had airstrips, most only accommodated small planes; those that did not have airstrips had to be accessed by seaplanes. I knew that much, though I was unaware of the limitations of the Dutch Harbor airfield at that time – thankfully.

My acceptance of the present situation still left plenty of room for doubt about what I had gotten myself into. My parents, upon learning about my decision to take their two grandchildren thousands of miles from Overland Park, Kansas, to a tiny island that was not even a dot on the map, were unsupportive to say the least. I was determined to prove them wrong, to prove we could stay in touch and visit occasionally. However, I didn't really believe that, and they probably didn't either. I had spent most of my teenage years in quiet defiance of the stable ordinary life they had planned for me. It was MY life and I'd had many a losing argument about what I wanted to do with it. Finally, at age twenty I made my break. That was seven years ago when I left, first for New Mexico and then on to Alaska in 1958 to teach school in Seward. But leaving the mainland, and not just for any island but one inhabited by only one other family did make me feel a little uneasy. I could understand my parents' concern. Should I have listened to them? I would soon find out.

I crossed the tarmac that afternoon with Malcolm's head pressed into my shoulder as I held him to me with one arm, and tightly gripped Becky's hand in mine. My head was bent almost to my chest as I attempted to avoid the tiny needles of sleet that stung my face. If it had been a sunny day I might have found my situation exciting, maybe a little scary, but after hauling my two kids and myself through gusts of wind and the biting sleet, I failed to enjoy the thrill of the moment. All I could think of was, what was I doing here? I strapped Becky in the seat right across the aisle from me, close enough so that I could reach across to her arm rest. Then I got myself settled with Malcolm snuggled in my lap against my soft fur parka. Cold Bay – whoever named it must have arrived on a day such as this.

"Isn't it awfully windy to fly?" I ventured to ask the stewardess. I was already a little uneasy before she started her spiel about oxygen masks and how to inflate life vests.

She gave me a pleasant - probably practiced- smile. "This must be your first flight out the Chain. These are not unusual flying conditions out here." Well that was reassuring! "You might wait a long time for flat calm. Reeve Aleutian Airlines has the best pilots in the world; they'll get you there." Her words sounded like a mantra, memorized in flight attendant school, meant to create an aura of confidence for first timers like me. In time, I was to learn that every bit of it was true. I tried to relax as I leaned back in my seat with my arm around Malcolm in my lap, while Becky sat quietly across the aisle within arm's reach, just taking in the new surroundings.

However, not long after we were airborne I wondered if this was what being in a stunt plane might be like, something I had never had any desire to find out. With my own lunch sloshing around inside me I noticed the pale drawn expressions on the children. This was supposed to be a short flight, about an hour. I hoped they/we could just hang in there. I had a feeling that at least one of us might need a barf bag, so with my free hand I removed one from the pocket on the back of the seat in front of me - just in case.

As the late winter storm continued to toss the plane from side to side, then up and down, the inevitable happened. Malcolm made gurgling sounds. When he raised his head I thought, here it comes, and moved the open paper bag under his chin. He took no time at all to fill it to capacity. Without coming up for air, he continued to empty the remaining contents of his stomach all over my new parka – I had only owned it one month - and of course, all over my hair. I sure didn't remember him having eaten that much.

With my hands full holding her miserable crying brother, his cheeks streaked with vomit and tears, I could not help Becky. It wouldn't have mattered anyway as she wouldn't have bothered with a bag, since she was into projectile vomiting at that time. Over the roar of the engines the stewardess yelled an apology at me for being unable to leave her seat and go to my daughter's aide as the plane continued to bounce and tilt its way through the light falling snow and heavy gusts of wind. No apology was necessary as Becky was beyond help in her accumulating mess. If we ever got out of that plane I had the fleeting thought that they might have to hose it down, before letting any passengers go on board again.

After what seemed like much longer than the hour I had been assured the flight would take, I felt the plane drop altitude, different from the rocking and rolling. Then it turned in a circular motion. As the plane tilted downward on my side I thought I could make out a few tiny lights through what looked like small snowflakes. The plane continued to spiral downward when the young stewardess, strapped into her seat with her hands grasping the armrests, loudly announced, "We will now attempt a landing on Dutch Harbor."

That descriptive word was not lost on me. The Aleutian wind currents were still in control. Her words were meant to prepare the passengers: we would either be landing or we would not. At the time I felt only terror. But everything was happening so fast I had little opportunity – thank goodness - to dwell on those words before the plane experienced some sort of new turbulence that produced a violent jolt, and the small craft plunged downward. Just as quickly it shot upward with such force that our seatbelts were all that kept us from being tossed into the narrow aisle or banging our heads on the low ceiling. Through the open cockpit door, I saw with alarm that the pilots bounced so hard they actually cleared their seats.

One positive result, I no longer had to hold that almost-to-overflowing smelly paper bag. I didn't look for it, either. Even as we all caught our breath, the tough little plane - and tough pilots - made a second attempt to get us on the ground, and this time they succeeded. I let out a long breath, which I hadn't been aware I'd been holding, as there was an abrupt cessation of motion. Later I would note that the alarmingly short landing strip had a beach at either end and was located at the foot of Mt. Ballyhoo, a picturesque well-known small mountain. Welcome to Dutch Harbor!

My husband, Charlie, had been with the Standard Oil Company's plant in Seward, Alaska, for less than a year when they offered him the transfer to Dutch Harbor. We had been told it was a remote deserted island except for one other family, the manager's. There was also a large abandoned military base which took up most of the island. In their rather immediate need to fill the position with anyone adventurous (or foolish) enough to accept the challenge, they sort of glossed over the fact that the job was located in one of the stormiest places in the world. Not to mention, it was also almost a thousand air miles away from hospitals, stores, telephones, radios and television. They did offer him a raise, however.

After we discussed it I could tell he really wanted the opportunity. We had arrived in Alaska just ahead of statehood, while it was still a territory, so we were prepared for some inconveniences, what with the far distance from the lower forty-eight, and with transportation so limited. But we did have some misgivings because of our two young children. Standard Oil made it seem more acceptable when they guaranteed they would pay for any flight out due to medical emergencies, and added that there were two weekly flights going out of Dutch Harbor on a regular basis, so it sounded okay. 'They' had obviously never been to Dutch Harbor. Charlie went on ahead to scout things out, two months before the arrival of the children and me that late April afternoon. He had sort of warned me that the closer one got to Dutch Harbor the rougher the flight became, but not to worry.

Remnants of fear still lingered as I struggled down the wobbly steps in the semi-darkness, one arm wrapped tightly around my crying toddler as strong gusts blew sleet crystals in my face. Becky was directly behind me, going down the steps, and I felt guilty that I couldn't help her; I knew she had to be as miserable as her brother. Charlie approached us that snowy windy April afternoon, his face one big smile. I was just as glad to see him but not for reasons he may have thought. I quickly handed him his puke-covered screaming son, then went to help his unhappy-looking daughter whose new coat was covered in foul-smelling greenish slime. A generally upbeat kind of guy, my husband turned to me, happy to see his family, and said cheerily, "I hope you're going to like it here."

"It won't make a bit of difference," I practically yelled, in a voice mixed with pent-up fear, relief and a bit of anger, "I'll never leave!"

Over time, I saw that amazing little plane make quite a few of its scheduled four landings per week, two arriving from Cold Bay and two on its return trip after overnighting at Nikolski on Umnak Island, the next one over from us. Having complete confidence in it now, I even looked forward to taking a trip Outside to see what the world had been doing in my absence.

Chapter

# 2

# Settling In

Only Charlie and the Reeve Aleutian Airways station manager, Larry Shaishnikoff, who lived on the neighboring island of Unalaska, about a five minute boat ride away, made up the welcoming party. Thankfully, no one else was there to witness our reeking condition, though in my distraught state I probably wouldn't have noticed anyway. We climbed into the company truck in the semi-darkness and rode up a low hill to our new home. Through the wind-driven sleety snow I could make out lights from what appeared to be two houses across the street from each other, with no other lights visible in the surrounding area. As we got closer, Charlie pointed out a one story house that sat on a little knoll at the top of the rise.

"That's our new home." He tried to sound cheerful in spite of our chaotic arrival. On the lower side of the road a huge house with lights shining from several floors loomed through the semidarkness. "The manager, Val Beal, and his family live there, right across the street. They have a little girl four years old, same as you, Becky. You'll meet her tomorrow."

I think Charlie was trying to make her feel better but I knew he'd have to tell her all over again later. "We're the only two families on the island. The population was four but now that you're here it's climbed to seven."

Charlie went on and on in that upbeat vein but it was lost on the three of us. All I could think of was clean clothes.

Both children were quiet, probably exhausted, as we parked on the road in front of what was supposed to be our home for the next three years. I climbed down from the big International and handed Charlie his son. The light snow added to the stillness and obliterated my vision of what I would observe in the next day's light. I then helped Becky down and we headed up the steps to the one-story ranch, anxious to get inside to warmth and clean clothes.

After we peeled off our soiled clothes, washed up, and changed into fresh clothing, the three of us felt much better and began to take in our surroundings. Charlie gave us the tour, and then went over our new living situation with me, while Becky and Malcolm roamed through the rooms of our new house. There were three bedrooms so they would each have their own room, a first. Our home in Seward was much smaller, only one bedroom till Charlie turned the small porch into a bedroom for the children. As they explored the large ranch-style, Becky picked her room, though Malcolm's was actually a mirror image. Charlie hoped that having their own rooms would make it easier for them to accept this adjustment to an isolated life.

He told me that while our location was considered remote, we were less than a mile from the neighboring island of Unalaska. An Alaska Native village located on it was just five or ten minutes across the water and also went by the name of Unalaska. There were one hundred seventy people of Aleut decent and thirty Caucasians according to the 1960 census. Even though it was a small community, he said it had an elementary school, a post office, a Russian Orthodox Church and several small general stores with limited selections. I was starting to get a clearer picture of this location, better than my expectations. Now I just hoped it lived up to my newly revised, much more favorable picture of our new home.

Some things I already knew, that there were no medical facilities, for instance. Charlie had been told, however, that a local village woman was well trained in Anchorage to be the village health aide, and kept some medicines and supplies. As a registered nurse I felt my medical background and the presence of another trained person should be sufficient.

Charlie

I knew Charlie had lots more he would like to tell me, but I was rapidly running out of energy so I put an end to the briefing and helped Becky and Malcolm get settled for the night. We had spent many hours traveling and sitting in waiting rooms, hard on adults with small children, and even harder on small children.

When Charlie had left Seward for Dutch Harbor, the children and I flew to Overland Park, Kansas, to visit my parents. That had been my first plane ride, the second when we headed back to Anchorage to change to the smaller plane, the DC-6. Communication was difficult in 1961 so

Charlie had not exchanged much information, just that they got a lot of wind sometimes. In retrospect, I think it may have occurred to him that I might have just stayed in Kansas if he went into too much detail. He was probably right so I am thankful that he did not.

Charlie left for work the next morning just as I was beginning to wake up. I walked into the spacious living room, then to the line of front windows that looked down on the dock and the bay a half mile away. The house sat on the crest of a hill so I could see for quite a distance, though mostly toward the bay and hills beyond. But I was a bit startled to see so many structures crowded into the limited amount of land that my vision took in. I knew there was only one other family living there, but what I saw was a huge subdivision of dwellings made up of weather-grayed wood. What a strange site, I thought. Then I decided to check out our house. Now the kids would each have their own room, so Becky could not complain about Malcolm getting into her things, for starters. She had been an only child for almost three years, so a baby brother was an adjustment.

Isolated or not, I did not think we were in danger of starving after I saw the long narrow pantry stocked like a small grocery store, with many shelves, plus two almost full freezers. I had never seen so much food in a private home, much less owned more than my most immediate staples. Since we were about eight hundred miles from a city (Anchorage) Charlie had made sure we would have plenty of food to last awhile. He had told me we had to order by catalog from Seattle and well in advance. How was I supposed to plan meals that far ahead? But he really wanted this transfer and had tried to anticipate any of my objections, so any complaints about the food situation were out – well, except for getting used to powdered milk. That would be the day!

Late that morning the wind died down, so my only neighbors, the manager's wife Georgina, and her four year old daughter ventured across the road to meet us. She told us her daughter was called Cookie, her nickname. Surprisingly, Cookie also had red hair, just like Becky's. What are the odds that two-thirds of the children on the island would have the least common - about 15% - hair color? Becky and Malcolm were friendly outgoing children so their faces lit up when they saw her, happy to know they would have a playmate and that she was just a few months younger than Becky. The three of them headed for Becky's room which was still in a bit of disarray.

Georgina filled me in on some of the things about island living and the small village across the water. Like our family, their assignment was only temporary, and then they would be transferred elsewhere. Being sent to Dutch Harbor seemed akin to being sentenced to exile in Siberia in those days. If an employee survived the isolation, lack of facilities, heavy workload and stormy weather, he should make good company material. At that time Charlie had no further ambition; he liked the work. He hadn't enjoyed his year of teaching in Seward, trying to work with teenage boys that were more into fighting over girls than they were into academics. After all those years of college he told me he did not enjoy spending his time breaking up fights. Charlie actually preferred working with his hands compared to teaching rowdy teenagers, so he was much happier with his current form of employment.

Charlie had been told that one of the reasons the company offered him this transfer was that they preferred family men, so that it wouldn't be too lonely in a remote place for the three year assignment. Though I had just arrived and hadn't seen it yet, Charlie told me about the established village just a short boat ride from our island. My new acquaintance had seemed comfortably adjusted when she told me of some of the things to expect. I thought it might be because she knew she would be leaving in a few years, and her husband was a company man so being subject to transfer went along with that kind of job.

I would learn in time that there were other people who lived in the Aleutians Islands and considered it home, not just a temporary living assignment, though I didn't know at that time whether it was by choice or necessity. I received little information about this unusual place before I arrived. But I still needed more time to decide if this was the best decision for our family. Could I ever consider this island home? That question did not enter my mind that first twenty-four hours, though if someone had asked me I probably would have replied, "Of course not!"

Dutch Harbor, 1960s Abandoned Buildings

Chapter

# 3

# Ghost Island

Twenty years before our family arrived, Amaknak Island was already a well-established military base, commonly referred to as the Dutch Harbor Naval Base. It was complete with planes, ships, and submarines, plus tens of thousands of troops. During the early part of World War II it was shrouded in secrecy. Very few people had ever heard of this very small island off the Alaska Peninsula, before it suddenly blazed into national headlines in June of 1942. Twice that month the Imperial Japanese Navy carrier-based planes bombed the base and caused much loss of life. The bombs also destroyed or damaged planes, boats, oil storage tanks, and various other structures. Because many called the base Dutch Harbor, which is actually the name of the boat harbor where the dock is, the island soon became known by that name, and 'Amaknak' became just another casualty of the war.

After World War II came to an end, the military base was no longer needed. The Navy and the Army removed all personnel from the island and left in its wake an eerie post-apocalyptic scene containing hundreds of abandoned weathered gray buildings, the remnants of what had once been a bustling community to thousands of servicemen. There are many historical accounts regarding those attacks, so I am only referencing it to explain what I saw first-hand the day after my arrival in early April, 1961, less than nineteen years later.

With our country now in the midst of a new war back in 1961, once again Dutch Harbor would play a significant role in its defense. Threatening rhetoric between the United States and Russia had not reached the stage of repopulating our island with military personnel. But with the real possibility of a volatile situation erupting into actual warfare the US didn't want to endure any more 'surprise' attacks. Those Russian threats were not taken lightly by our government. It was a sad turn of events as they had been our allies in World War II against the Nazi regime but I suppose it was predictable on some level. With Alaska's vast western coastline only a few navigable miles from Russian lands geographically, my chosen state was their closest access to our country. Hence, the government's Distant Early Warning Line, known as the DEW Line, was put in place by the military utilizing RCA (Radio Corporation of America)'s communications technology along that coast, which included the Aleutian Islands.

Standard Oil of California leased Dutch Harbor from the Navy in the '50s to supply the fuel for the DEW Line operation, which stretched from the farthest Aleutian island site at Shemya, just before Attu, to the farthest north site above the Arctic Circle. Our family's arrival in such a strategic location in 1961 came right in the middle of such ongoing national tension. With somewhat limited communication to the Outside world, I was not fully aware of the danger surrounding our present home. I knew that there was a military base on Kodiak Island, just before the Chain began, because they performed medical rescues for our area. But the government didn't deem it necessary to send troops back to Dutch Harbor. I am glad the Russians were not aware that there was only a population of seven to defend it.

Many of the necessary facilities were already on Dutch Harbor, left by the Navy, including an oil tank farm, a dock and a few well-maintained houses. Some of the huge silver storage tanks still showed remnants of another war, scars of bullet holes where they had been strafed by the Japanese planes. Though they were serviceable, their repairs were still visible and gave some of them a misshapen look. The dock was long, and very wide, ideal for handling the huge tankers that came in, some as much as 600 to 700 feet long. They brought the oil all the way from California to Dutch Harbor to offload into those huge shiny storage tanks.

Empty barges driven by powerful tugboats came out of Washington and made the long and sometimes rough trip to Dutch Harbor to be filled with the stored petroleum products. The tugboats and barges then either made the long run to the end of the Aleutian Chain or way up North to the remote sites at the top of Alaska, sometimes having to go behind a Canadian icebreaker if winter ice packs had started to seal off all access up North.

Nineteen years after Dutch Harbor had been the scene of so much destruction, clusters of weathered structures, declared surplus then abandoned by the military, still remained. Their unpainted appearance, often without doors and usually windowless, resembled a ghost town, drab and forlorn, and stressed the bleakness of Dutch Harbor. I could only see some of them from my living room window that first day. There was light snow on some roofs but it could not hide their lonely appearance. A feeling of sadness came over me. I had lived through WWII but had experienced it from the distance of a childhood in the mid-west experiencing the rationing and deprivations, and darkened windows at night. But seeing what I observed that first morning brought the reality of it home to me. A war had taken place here, bombs were dropped and people died.

When Charlie came home for lunch that first day he filled me in a little more. I commented on how large and roomy our house was and he told me it had been a naval officer's residence. He said that except for the manager's house it was the second largest house on the island. Then he told me that there were three houses just past ours that Standard Oil also maintained. They were set up as bunkhouses for occasional visiting work crews. So those five houses were the only ones that they renovated, the only ones that were painted. Those white structures stood out amid the gray drab wood of the dilapidation surrounding us.

When the weather was tolerable and Charlie had the time, he took the children and me to explore some of the hundreds of dark deserted buildings, armed with flashlights. Knowing the former inhabitants had lived here under difficult circumstances – and some had died here - helped us to realize a little of what those soldiers, sailors, and marines must have endured. The true name for the island, Amaknak, was given by a Russian in the eighteen hundreds. Its meaning is 'burial place', a fitting name for that silent and lonely island in the early sixties.

I had naturally never lived in such a strange place, one that showed some remnants of a horrific war, looking like something from a black and white newsreel, no people, just empty damaged structures.

The island was designated a military base so it was like a city unto itself, complete in its own way. The buildings we went through were often stripped bare, perhaps from scavengers, but we could usually make out what they had been. Even in its aged condition one large dilapidated structure was obviously a mess hall/movie theater combination. The hospital, gym, bakery, and bowling alley were some of the obvious ones. And there was no question about what one really unique find was with its iron bars and a lever that locked all the doors simultaneously, which incidentally still worked. The post office with its many rows of wooden slots was an easy one to recognize also. It probably handled as much mail as a medium sized town, considering the many thousands of men that went through there. An interesting structure was a fire station which still had the fire man's pole in it, though in later years it found its way over to the village of Unalaska.

In a lot of the buildings the interior walls were damaged from the frequent wind storms that howled through broken windows, driving in sheets of rain. Some roofs had been ripped off, though the many that were intact helped preserve the buildings so that they could be refurbished. Quonset huts were as common as dandelions on a lawn. They were of a somewhat prefab nature, allowing them to be constructed quickly but also more prone to the destructive forces of the hurricane-like winds, leaving uprooted corrugated piles of debris scattered about that windswept treeless island. With no one to clean up the rusting accumulation, it contributed to that mostly abandoned look of the island.

Once after climbing over a collapsed sheetrock wall we discovered remnants of letters, partially shredded. Probably the many squirrels that overran the island were responsible. Sometimes we saw scribbles on the still-existing barracks walls. In the men's quarters a sign that had survived warned 'No Horseplay in Barracks'. I would have thought those men would have torn that one down at the first opportunity.

Charlie ventured into the attic of one of the buildings and found components of a home brew operation. There were boxes of recycled bottles, a bottle capper, boxes of caps and a few miscellaneous items. Neither of us had any experience in the brewery department but we found a resource in talking with some of our new friends across the water. As it turned out, it was a rather common beverage since there was not a liquor store in the town. All alcohol was shipped by plane from Anchorage. After we sent for the necessary ingredients we made our first batch. I discovered ours had a very yeasty taste. I did not much care for liquid bread. But Charlie took it on for a while, trying to improve on the flavor. With his limited free time, however, that new hobby was short lived. Actually finding that stash was yet another reminder to me of what military life must have been like for those young men stationed in a place so different and remote.

Of a more ominous nature, we observed the grave evidence of the remnants of the danger which that small island faced, viewed as a stepping-stone to the US mainland by the enemy. Military structures included anti-aircraft and artillery gun emplacements on hilltops. The hillsides were dotted with concrete bunkers. Pillboxes were still in place along the beach placed there to guard the shore line. All were grim reminders to us that this was not in fact a sleepy small town military base with housing and such amenities as a theater and a bowling alley. Amaknak Island was located on the front lines of battle and prepared to defend American territory.

The many military roads made exploring the low hillsides and rocky beaches easy. Charlie told me what all those structures were for since I had a very limited knowledge of anything military, whereas he had fought in Korea less than ten years before. Becky and Malcolm had little if any understanding of wars at that time, but later they would remember those structures and also remember climbing inside the concrete bunkers, which were like tiny playhouses to them – everything is relevant.

Looking back on that life, I realize that we had been living in the midst of an historical site, like Gettysburg or Custer's Last Stand. Though some of its importance has been lost with the passage of time, soldiers had died here serving and protecting their country, warding off an enemy invasion on U.S. soil.

1962, Abandoned Military Base, Dutch Harbor

Chapter

# 4

# Trip to Anchorage

After we were comfortably settled in, Georgina invited us to have lunch with her and Cookie as the men would not be home for lunch with all the dock traffic going on. She used that opportunity to take me through the exquisite two story house with its fully finished basement that she told me was referred to as the 'Admiral's' House'. Whether it was or was not, I don't know, but Charlie had told me that our two houses had belonged to the highest ranking Naval Officers stationed there. Besides the very large rooms, the Admiral's House had oak floors and bannisters throughout, a fireplace with a mantel, a spacious dining room, separate breakfast room, four bathrooms, three bedrooms on the second floor and one in the maid's quarters in the basement. That house was like a castle among the rubble.

In late spring activity on the dock picked up and was a very busy time for the guys, but provided lots of overtime. Charlie was either pumping out the tankers or pumping fuel into barges. The two men from the village of Unalaska, Walter Dyakanoff and Carl Moller, worked full time year-round on Dutch Harbor. They made the short five or ten minute trip between the two islands every day. Sometimes extra help from the village was hired during the busy season.

Charlie, Walter, and Carl also had other duties besides the dock. They kept the airport runway in shape and fueled the planes. In addition, they maintained the multiple dirt-and-gravel roads that crisscrossed the island, put in by the military many years before. Two huge generators located in a large workshop about a few blocks down from our house, and just up from the airstrip provided power for the whole island. Sometimes in severe windstorms the power got knocked out and the men would have to do the repairs. Charlie was the most knowledgeable regarding anything electrical, so much of the maintenance fell to him. His Industrial Arts major back in college proved useful on that do-it-yourself island, hundreds of miles from repair shops.

In the midst of all that first summer's activity I realized I was expecting a baby. Charlie and I were very excited as we wanted a big family. He was the youngest of ten and had enjoyed having lots of siblings around.

I planned to go to Anchorage when I was close to my due date, but I had no reservations about bringing a baby back to this remote area. Many of the women in the village had their babies at home, though some did go in to the Anchorage hospital. The babies I had observed seemed to be doing just fine. I knew it was a little chancy, though, with the limited medical facilities available, especially if anything went wrong. I had spent a lot of time working as a delivery room nurse, both in Kansas City and in New Mexico, before moving to Alaska. There is never a way to predict which delivery will result in serious complications so I wanted a hospital delivery.

I had just written a letter to my parents telling them they would be grandparents again and put it in the outgoing mailbag. The plane from Cold Bay had come in that afternoon and went on to overnight at the next stop, Nikolski. My letter would go out on its return flight to Dutch Harbor on the way back to Cold Bay, then on the DC-6 to Anchorage. I did not know I would also be on that plane when I put my letter in the mail drop.

Late that afternoon, after the plane had left for Nikolski, I started bleeding. In a short time it slowed to just spotting which I knew did not always result in a miscarriage. I'd had bleeding, though mostly spotting, for a while with my first child, Becky, yet went on to full term and delivered a perfectly

Admiral's House

healthy baby. Realistically, though, I knew it could go either way and was not something to be taken lightly.

I had Charlie make contact with the Anchorage doctor I had written to earlier to be my obstetrician when it was close to time for me to deliver. He told Charlie to have me take the next plane out and then take a cab from the airport at Anchorage to Providence Hospital. On my arrival they would notify him. And he would see me there. Everything was happening so fast, so much to do in such a short time.

This was Charlie's first summer at Dutch Harbor and it was in the middle of the busy season. When the Reeve Aleutian plane showed up the next morning, Charlie was already at work. The manager's wife agreed to look after Becky and Malcolm, and the children were happy about that arrangement.

The girls were practically inseparable, and they accepted Malcolm as a tag-a-long. Actually, he fit in pretty well, for still being a toddler.

My trip to Anchorage, which involved taking the usual two planes, was uneventful. We had good flying weather, unlike my previous flight from Cold Bay to Dutch Harbor. Upon my arrival, I took a cab to the hospital emergency room as I had been told, and the staff notified my doctor.

After checking me he said, "You can stay at a hotel cheaper than the hospital while waiting to see what develops. Call me if your symptoms escalate. Just try and rest as much as possible."

I appreciated that. Even with insurance a hotel would still cost a lot less. It was 1961 in Anchorage and oil had yet to create the massive explosion of expensive high-rise hotels, so most of them were pretty cheap.

I took a cab to the old Roosevelt Hotel downtown. I rented a room for five dollars a night, complete with fiberboard walls that showed dots of light like stars in a dark sky when my light was turned off and the next room's light was on. While that hotel has since been torn down with the sudden expansion of the city, it was not unique at the time. This was still frontier Alaska. I stayed in bed most of the time and just read books, hoping it was a false alarm, and was even making some long-range plans. But on the fourth day of what had been minimal bleeding, there was a sudden and frightening gush of blood. With a sinking feeling, I hurriedly called the doctor.

"Take a cab to the hospital immediately and I'll meet you in the emergency room," he said. The 'wait and see' was over, and I knew I had lost.

I tried to remain calm as I sat silently in the cab, after telling the driver to take me to the Providence Hospital Emergency Room. My eyes felt hot as I held back tears while I held a small paper package to give to the doctor. To the uninitiated, it was just a bloody blob, but to me it was very real.

Upon my arrival, the doctor was already there. After examining the bloody package, he confirmed the inevitable, the remains of a tiny human being. The doctor then did a procedure to stop the continuous bleeding.

"I want you to remain in the hospital for a few days to be sure you're okay. You have lost a lot of blood and you will be returning to an isolated location with limited facilities. I'll check on you in the morning."

The hospital would one day go the way of my hotel room with its star-lights, both later demolished and replaced with huge modern structures. But when I was admitted back in 1961 I was placed in a four-bed ward with only white curtains to separate the patients. The bed was an old fashioned white iron bed with perpendicular spokes for a headboard. Lying there, I saw some cracks in the aging plaster, and that was pre-Alaska earthquake.

Only looking back do I see the room; at the time my thoughts were on the loss I had just sustained. The medication I had been given to help calm me had worn off by that night. I was suddenly overcome with the reality that there was not going to be a baby – one that we had anticipated with joy and excitement. I began to sob hysterically, uncontrollably. I was oblivious to the three other women patients sharing the room, though I could hear them talking to each other in the background, complaining about the noise I was making. So I guess I wasn't totally oblivious, just unable to control the disruption I was causing. A nurse appeared and gave me a shot. She said it would relax me and help me get to sleep. Possibly one of the other patients had called the nurse. That shot would also help them get some sleep.

When the doctor visited me the next day, he said, "You appear to be doing okay and there is no bleeding so I am going to discharge you, but I think you should remain in Anchorage for a few days. I just want to be sure you are doing okay before going back to Dutch Harbor."

I checked out of the hospital and took a cab back to the Roosevelt to wait for the next Reeve Aleutian plane. I just wanted to get back home to my family. My roommates were probably happy to see me go, but I was over my crying jag. A quiet resignation had settled in. I was still young, twenty-nine at the time. There would surely be other children.

Party at the Beals – Cookie, Becky, Joan

Chapter

# 5

# First Summer

*Upon returning* to Dutch Harbor, again on uneventful flights, I just buried my pain and got on with the challenges and adventures that the island presented, and was thankful for the children I had.

On some rare days when it was neither raining nor too windy, Becky, Malcolm and I, plus Cookie sometimes, roamed the rugged shores looking for sea treasures. Storm-driven waves tossed Japanese glass net floats high onto the rocky island beaches, littering them with those transparent green and blue balls that came in several sizes. The commonest, the small green ones, were not much bigger than a tennis ball. Others were about the size of a sandwich plate, while the most prized, so naturally least common, were the ones as big as basketballs, reminding me of lawn ornaments. Besides the large ones being special, so were the pale blue balls with netting still on them. They were my favorites,

Joan

though we did manage to find a few – very few- of the basketball-size ones over the years, my second favorites.

Beach jewels – at least that was our name for them - were another treasure that we gathered. They were nothing more than broken glass worn smooth by the incessant wave action. Those gray shores sparkled in shades of amber, green, cobalt, white and occasionally red. We placed them in glass jars in our front windows to catch the sunlight, or at least the light. The small glass balls and various kinds of shells joined them to give our front room quite a nautical look.

On other days, when the weather was good on Charlie's days off, we went across the bay to visit the village of Unalaska. We had a small open wooden boat that he had purchased from the employee that he had replaced. When we got over there, we walked everywhere. Back in 1961, there were few vehicles in use on the narrow gravel village roads and most places were within easy walking distance anyway. Fortunately the town was pretty flat. I enjoyed just walking the creek road and meeting people along the way. Everyone was very friendly. Though we were newcomers, they seemed to welcome us into their community and they made us feel comfortable there. I did not feel any of the loneliness that I had anticipated, quite the opposite. I was very happy there.

There were three stores along the main road in the village that summer. The Alaska Commercial Company, the largest, carried a variety of goods, from groceries to hardware though all in limited supply. It was a historical structure, one of a chain of Alaska-based stores that had a history going back to the year 1716. Alaska was owned by Russia and trading posts were set up under the name Russian-American Trading Company. When Russia sold Alaska to the United States in 1867 the stores were purchased by several men from California and the name was changed. When we arrived in 1961 it was in the process ofbeing sold to Carl Moses, part Alaska Native, who spent some of the year in Juneau as a state politician. By the summer's end the historic name would be changed to Carl's Commercial.

The second largest store, Aleutian Mercantile, was owned by an older non-Alaska Native bachelor, Pop Horton, that everyone called Pops. It carried mostly groceries and was closest to the elementary school. During the lunch hour the students often went there to purchase snacks since the school didn't have a lunch program back then.

The third store was the smallest by comparison and carried mostly produce, but also some other groceries. The owner was a local fisherman, Verne Robinson, a non- Alaska Native who was married to a local Aleut woman, Mary. Each had existing families from previous marriages plus they were the joint parents of three pre-school children when we arrived in 1961. Verne told us he had to keep plenty of groceries on hand for their large family so he might as well have his own grocery store. In later years he would purchase Aleutian Mercantile when Pops retired and moved Outside.

I became more familiar with catalog shopping, however, so I no longer needed a real store to remind me of the world I had left behind. I made those trips across the water primarily to visit some of the people I had become acquainted with. Our casual relationships rapidly grew into strong friendships. We often exchanged dinner invitations with some of our new friends, equating the short expanse of water as no more of an obstacle than to driving a mile down a road to visit someone. Dutch Harbor soon began to feel like home, even with its strange surroundings, as I quickly adjusted to the opportunities and limitations of our new life. Bonding in isolation became a perk that is sometimes lacking in larger communities.

Chapter

# 6

# Movies and Whales

I've already mentioned that I grew up in the Kansas City, Missouri area, a vast Midwest metropolis of multiple high-rises, concrete sidewalks, magnificent parks, and the overall feeling of a prosperous, expanding city. Going to one of the downtown movie theaters was an event in itself. Some of the theaters were architectural wonders with their outstanding exterior features and their lavish interiors. An excellent example was the Loew's Midland Theater, built back in the late twenties, supposedly at a cost of over four million dollars. Upon entering the building, that figure was easy to believe. Movie-goers enjoyed the sight and comfort of the very beautiful plush carpeting, and were led by a uniformed usher to one of the three thousand five hundred velvet-covered seats where they relaxed in comfort and watched first-run movies, the latest out of Hollywood. When I attended a movie at one of those theaters I usually dressed up, or at least didn't wear old or dirty clothes; however, that was a part of my past that I left behind.

In the main part of town at Unalaska there was an ordinary-looking two-story building. The first floor served as a place for occasional parties and community dances. Once a week, on Saturday night, the second floor was used to show old black and white 16mm films. Besides the large white screen, there were backless wooden benches, a projector and a popcorn machine. My friends, Gert and Sam Svarny, operated the theater, known as the Williwaw, for Gert's sister, Lillie Hope, who was not at Unalaska the time we were. During intermission while the reel was being changed, Gert and her young daughters handled the popcorn concession and the movie-goers spent time visiting with one another.

Often on Saturday mornings I anxiously watched the weather situation, observing the bay and the strength of the wind while standing outside my front door. I interrogated Charlie about his work schedule, such as, were any boats due at the fuel dock that day. Saturdays had become important to me, the evenings, actually. When the water was calm enough and Charlie wasn't working, we made the short trip across the water in our open wooden boat, ignoring the darkness and cold and the frequent light rain, plus some frozen patches in winter. After we reached the creek that ran along one of the main dirt roads, Charlie found some protrusion in the low bank and tied up the boat while the kids and I climbed out. Then the four of us scrambled awkwardly up the often muddy dirt bank to the road – Charlie often carrying Malcolm. We then had a short walk to the Williwaw. By the time we arrived our heavy clothes were frequently damp and sometimes muddy, but no one seemed to notice, often calling friendly greetings like "We're glad you made it." We felt welcome there.

We settled on one of the backless wood benches in the dark and enjoyed old black and white movies, often ones that we had seen years ago and which now had become classics. We never got tired of seeing those old movies. Maybe it was a nostalgia thing. Maybe it was the camaraderie of watching with friends - probably both. All the grandeur of the big city theaters was now lost to me. Their beauty and amenities could not compete with what I had discovered on this tiny little sparsely populated island - my favorite outing, movie night at the Svarny Theater.

In a very short time we formed a close friendship with the Svarnys. I learned that Gert was a gifted Native Alaskan Unangan artist, skilled in working with various media, such as bone, ivory, soapstone and wood. I was amazed at the beautiful and very professional quality of what I saw, seemingly buried away in a small isolated village. But with time others would become aware of her special talents and she would hold a reputation as one of the finest Native Alaskan artists in the state.

Gert and Sam Sarny

As for Sam, he was not just 'the artist's husband'. Sam was an Army sergeant and a veteran of WWII, stationed on Unalaska to be in charge of the RCA office, the building that included a huge marine radio for the village. Though in the Army and subject to the usual military transfers, Sam chose to make his permanent home at Unalaska, his wife's home town, and raise his family there whenever he could.

Charlie and I enjoyed many dinners with our new friends, sometimes at their home, sometimes at ours, as we became increasingly comfortable with our new life. Nothing was as I had expected, and that was a good thing.

In the midst of the many new things that I experienced that summer, I saw my first whale and it was very close up. Its huge carcass was about forty feet long and lying on its side in shallow water on the beach near the Standard Oil dock, condition D.O.A. Charlie, the kids and I headed down there with our little black and white Polaroid camera, for what we considered an experience of a lifetime. To the locals it was not a novelty – rather, a source of food. If you have never seen one of those sea monsters, it is a fascinating sight – even if it is dead. When we arrived near the beach, about six blocks downhill from our house, several skiffs were alongside the dead creature. A few men from the village were butchering away on the carcass.

Butchering Whale near Dutch Harbor Shore

I'd never eaten — or seen — whale meat but watching huge heavy chunks being removed made me think that it must be very tasty to some people. Previously I had associated whale meat with the Eskimos of the Far North, so much for that myth!

A newcomer to Alaska is often referred to by old-timers as a cheechako (greenhorn), but I had thought I had 'graduated', what with all of my so-called new experiences. This is such a vast state, though, and so much was different for me from what I was familiar with in the lower '48 – like watching a whale being cut up into slabs of meat practically on my doorstep. The cold temperature of the water helped to preserve it for a little while, a few days at least, but that soon came to a smelly end.

After several days, a massive chunk of flesh was missing out of the whale's side. The men quit going to the site and we were left with a rotting mammal on our hands - well, on our beach. The foul odor had already begun to drift up the road toward my front door. The men working on the dock knew the obnoxious smell would only get stronger, making for very unpleasant working conditions. A tugboat was there at the time so they requested that it pull the decaying monster away from the dock area and out to sea. Since that boat also had to be at the dock the captain was greatly motivated to be of assistance.

Just as the tugboat pulled away headed for deep water with the foul-smelling mammal in tow, it was met by an incoming Standard Oil tanker. On arrival at the dock, the Captain of the tanker jokingly reported to Charlie that they had encountered a tugboat which was not flying the right signals for towing a 'submerged article'.

Chapter

7

# First Christmas – Visitors

Our only neighbors on Dutch Harbor left for a Christmas vacation that December of '61 so we were prepared for a very quiet, somewhat lonely holiday celebration. We did not expect to have a Christmas tree as we had not thought to order one in advance. We were still in the learning stages of living in isolation. Trees were not native to the island, with only a few scattered evergreens planted by traders or servicemen years ago, struggling to survive the harsh Aleutian storms. Then, to our surprise, Standard Oil sent us a Christmas tree on the plane. Becky, Malcolm and I made little decorations for it and for our front room, though we didn't expect anyone to enjoy them except the four of us.

On Christmas Eve we settled down to await the only visitor we were expecting, Santa Claus. Later that evening from our front windows we spotted the lights of a very large ship approaching the bay. Since Charlie had not received word that Standard Oil was sending a tanker during the holidays, it was a puzzling sight as it entered the bay and then simply anchored there. It was too far away and too dark to make it out, so we were left to wonder who our visitor might be.

What had started out earlier to be a quiet family Christmas Eve was further disrupted after we had just gone to bed and settled Becky and Malcolm down for the night, telling them Santa would not show up till they were asleep. Just as we ourselves had started to doze off Charlie got a call from the hand-cranked phone on Unalaska that a small boy was very ill with a high fever and the health aide was in Anchorage. Would I go check on him if they sent a boat over to get me? It was close to midnight but I knew how overly cautious all of us were when it came to sickness as we were hundreds of miles from doctors and hospitals. Of course I agreed to go, though our children were too young to leave alone.

There was always a truck left at the boat landing, so whoever came across used it to come by the house to pick me up. The channel sometimes froze over during the winter and it was frozen over that night. To get across, the boat had to act as an ice breaker. The man operating the skiff ran the bow up on top of the frozen channel, then rocked it till it broke through, which made for slow going. Fortunately, our open wooden boats were pretty sturdy. To add to our difficulties on that night, the snow was falling thick and fast, creating a whiteout, as we felt our way across the channel. There were times when it was hard for me to see the end of the skiff. Fortunately, it was a very narrow crossing. Traveling on the ice was not a new experience for me as Charlie had already done that a few times when we wanted to get across on movie night.

When I entered the village it was just after midnight. We walked down the dark deserted snowy road to the home of the young boy who was ill. Through the falling snow I could make out the glow from the lights of that huge ship still looming off in the distance, an unusual sight. The rest of the night I spent sponging, hydrating, and medicating the young child in an effort to get his fever down with what there was available to work with. Occasionally, I was able to take cat naps in a chair while one of the women staying there took over. By morning his fever broke and he was resting quietly so I was given a ride back to Dutch, a much easier journey in spite of the ice breaker routine as the snow had stopped, though it was still dark. I made it home just after Becky and Malcolm had gotten up and had seen presents under the tree. They were happy to see me, mainly because Charlie told them they couldn't open anything till I got back. That sick little boy got better just in time to make two little children happy; I don't know how much longer Charlie could have held them off.

Later that Christmas morning the big ship, the size of a tanker, pulled into the dock. It was obviously a foreign ship but there wasn't much light yet to make it out clearly. So Charlie drove down to the dock to check on it. He returned a while later to let me know what was going on as he knew I was just as curious.

"It's a Greek freighter and the captain said their ship developed mechanical troubles so they need to do some repairs before they can continue their journey," Charlie told me. "He has his wife on board with him and they seem like really friendly people. Since it is Christmas Day I took the liberty of inviting them for dinner. I didn't think you'd mind."

"Of course not. I'll bet they would like to get off of the boat for a while. It'll be fun visiting with people from another country." We loved getting visitors. We did not see many people in our isolation, and they did not have to be foreigners, but I thought that would be a plus. "I am already fixing a big turkey dinner, anyway, so there is plenty to share. I will just lie down for a little while to catch up on some rest since Becky and Malcolm are pretty well occupied right now.

When our guests arrived, the captain was wearing a fancy dark uniform, just like I pictured a captain of a big ship would wear. His wife was quite attractive, looking elegant in a black sheath dress, her jet black hair pulled back in a bun. Both were friendly and talkative, and spoke excellent English. We learned much about that ancient country of Greece, from agriculture to politics.

After dinner, as they prepared to leave, we exchanged gifts and we might have anyway. But it was more significant because it was Christmas Day, not just our holiday but theirs, too. One of the presents that I gave the captain's wife was an Alaskan cookbook. However, I doubt she found much use back in Athens for recipes on preparing jellied moose nose and bear steak! Actually, I didn't either. We only had squirrels on Dutch Harbor. It is hard to celebrate such a special holiday without others to share it with you.

As 1961 on Dutch Harbor approached the new year, I looked back at the many 'firsts' I had encountered since leaving behind all the advantages, comforts, and pleasures of city living. Very soon after my arrival in that remote and sparsely populated spot off the coast of Alaska, and despite my initial misgivings, I had fallen under the spell of the Aleutians and had no thoughts of wanting to live elsewhere. Charlie was affected in the same way and did not like to think about what he would do when his contract was up in three years. Neither did I. How differently we both felt after less than a year in a place that couldn't be more opposite from the towns and cities we had left behind. Had we been dropped off in Never-Never land?

1962, Abandoned Military Base, Dutch Harbor

Chapter

# 8

# Minneapolis Tribune

Twice a week the Reeve Aleutian plane dropped off mail in canvas duffle bags, weather permitting. The bulk of it was headed for the Unalaska Post Office, but there was always at least one bag labeled Dutch Harbor, sometimes more. A certain amount was Standard Oil business plus some personal mail and lots of catalogs and 'junk' mail. Isolated as I was in so many respects, I enjoyed getting mail of any kind. Occasionally, I received pen-pal requests and if they were from school children I gave them to teachers in Unalaska for their students. If they were from adults, I answered them, which resulted in a few close and very interesting long-term pen-pals.

That first fall of 1961 a letter arrived from the Arts Editor of the Minneapolis Star and Tribune, John K. Sherman. Like so many others it was addressed generically to anybody at Dutch Harbor. His request was a little different from the ones looking for pen–pals. He collected postcards, and wanted one from Dutch Harbor. I wrote him that there was no town or post office at Dutch Harbor, described the island's present condition and inhabitants and explained that the nearest post office was in a small – really small - village on the island of Unalaska, about a five or ten minute boat ride from us.

THE MINNEAPOLIS STAR
*Evening*
AND
THE MINNEAPOLIS TRIBUNE
*Morning and Sunday*

JOHN K. SHERMAN
ARTS EDITOR

Feb. 12, 1962

Dear Mrs. Brown:

I appreciated your Christmas greeting from far-off Dutch Harbor, and I hope you write again.

I suggested to our Sunday Editor here that a story written by you about the only family at Dutch Harbor might make interesting reading in our Sunday travel section. Would you care to take it on? He thought it was a good idea. Write it informally, just like a letter, and if you have nice contrasty photos that would reproduce well, showing Dutch Harbor and the Browns, could you loan them to us?

One more request! When you write again, will you use the enclosed envelope or one similar? I want to get that Unalaska postmark in my collection on an envelope small enough for my pages.

Best regards,

John K. Sherman

Letters from John Sherman, Arts

THE MINNEAPOLIS STAR
*Evening*
AND
THE MINNEAPOLIS TRIBUNE
*Morning and Sunday*

JOHN K. SHERMAN
ARTS EDITOR

April 9, 1962

Dear Joan Brown:

I want to thank you for the script and also for the small envelope I neglected to enclose in my last. The story is a corking good one, the Sunday editor is highly pleased with it and intends to use it in a forthcoming issue, even sending a modest check which of course you can't use, having nowhere to spend it.

People here no longer laugh at my foolish hobby when it produces byproducts like this. I'll see that you get a tearsheet of the story when it's printed: it may be a month or two yet. Spring is here now, although it has the Alaskan touch yet.

Best regards & thanks,

John K. Sherman

Letters from John Sherman, Arts

Dutch Harbor had become very well known as a result of World War II, so John Sherman was determined to come up with something for his collection. He asked me to take and send him a few pictures of the island or something of interest there. Then he would make them into postcards and return my originals. He would include some copies to send back to him with the Unalaska post mark, plus a few extra for me. The only camera we had was a cheap Polaroid which was one of the first that came out and made only very small rectangular black and white pictures. I had Charlie take a few pictures of the dead whale on our beach that was being butchered and some of Dutch Harbor itself in its abandoned state. In spite of the 'inexpensive' photography – nothing National Geographic would ever accept – John Sherman must have been satisfied. Very shortly I received some nice looking 'Dutch Harbor' postcards, probably the result of some professional studio work. Later, I sent him a Christmas card with a thank you note for the extras he had sent me and I thought that was the end of our correspondence.

Late in February of 1962 I received another letter from John Sherman, again with an unusual request. This time it was not postcards and postmarks. He wrote that he had suggested to his Sunday Editor that I write a story about our life on Dutch Harbor to be put in the Sunday travel section of the Minneapolis Tribune. The editor thought it was a good idea. John Sherman asked that I also enclose a few more Dutch Harbor pictures and make sure the envelope would have the Unalaska post mark. Normally I put all my outgoing mail in the Dutch Harbor mail bag and it would be postmarked in Anchorage. Considering how big the world is, with its many countries, cities and towns, he could end up with a huge collection, unless he placed some limitations. But he did not seem to have any limitations for Alaska, and for that I was thankful.

I was flattered and happy to oblige his editor's request as I already enjoyed writing family and friends about my new life and its uniqueness. As Charlie and I were becoming increasingly drawn to life in the Aleutians, I was glad to be given an opportunity to share my experiences with a much broader audience and wanted them to see it through my eyes.

In the fall of '62 John Sherman sent me a thank you letter stating "the story had made quite a splash" and they thought it was "splendid". Then a few weeks later, I received a small check from the newspaper along with an Alaskan novel that he wanted me to write a review on. He would have the review published and again send me a small check. He always referred to them as small checks and in fact they were – small enough to keep me from getting a 'big head'. Since reading and writing have always been my favorite pastimes, I would have done it for nothing.

The Minneapolis Tribune published my story as a full front page article in their Sunday Travel Feature section later that year. It was so long and included a couple of pictures that the rest of my story was continued on a different page.

In response to the article, I received letters from a variety of people. The majority were from soldiers or their wives. The men wrote about their personal experiences while stationed at Dutch Harbor. One told of enduring the bombing raid and having had some of his friends killed during the attack. Mostly though, the letters thanked me for letting them know what had become of Dutch Harbor after the military pulled out. The wife of one of the men even sent me a present of several couch pillows she had made, a sort of thank you for writing it. I had not thought of that angle when I wrote it and had not considered that ex-GIs who had been on Dutch Harbor back then were living in the Minneapolis area and would see that particular article. In some ways it made me feel as if I were not so far away and cut off from the rest of the country.

Not all of the letters I received were from ex-soldiers who had spent time there. Some letters were from individuals that just liked to read stories about Alaska, just like John Sherman. The most unique one was from a Minnesota man in his sixties, Jim Robieson (not a misspelling) who wrote how the story brought back memories about his unresolved dream of going to Alaska that went back to his early single days. What was different about the letter was its long detailed narrative, four typed single-spaced pages full of family information and revealed longing. I was so touched by it that I wrote him back in kind, giving much more background about myself than I had in the article. This resulted in a lengthy correspondence that lasted till his death about nine years later. His wife then sent me a gracious letter informing me that he had died. She requested that I continue writing as

THE MINNEAPOLIS STAR
*Evening*
AND
THE MINNEAPOLIS TRIBUNE
*Morning and Sunday*

JOHN K. SHERMAN
ARTS EDITOR

Oct. 10, 1962

Dear Joan (pardon the familiarity):

Herewith a few tearsheets of your story, which made quite a splash and which I and others here thought was splendid. I hope you continue to write from time to time, even if not for publication, so that I can keep apprised of Dutch Harbor doings.

Wallace Allen, our Sunday editor, is going to send you a little check which will keep the wolf from your door for about five minutes at least. Let me know if this doesn't reach you in a reasonable length of time. Wally, who liked your story and asked me to get it from you in the first place, has a cancerous spot on his lung and is going to St. Barnabas Hospital here shortly. He is one of our finest men, an imaginative, enterprising but gentle soul, and I am worried about him.

It has been such a rat race here since the strike ended that I've had no time for hobbies. Soon though I'm going to get some postcards printed from your negatives and send them to you.

Best regards,

John K. Sherman

Letters from John Sherman, Arts

she had always read my letters and enjoyed hearing about my life. She took up the correspondence where Jim left off, even after she entered a nursing home a few years later. When she died in the early 1970s one of her daughters notified me and for a little while longer she and her sister continued to correspond with me. I feel that I owe those unforgettable friendships that spanned almost two decades to the article and John Sherman's initial inquiry.

While John Sherman and I continued to communicate with each other for a few more years, eventually it came to an end. I didn't know why at the time but I later learned that he had died of a heart attack in his office the day before his seventy-first birthday, in 1969. He had worked for the Minneapolis Star–Tribune for almost thirty years, covering the cultural front. Music apparently was a special favorite of his as he had written several books on the subject. By giving me a taste of journalism, he fulfilled one of my childhood dreams.

1962, Abandoned Military Base, Dutch Harbor

Chapter

# 9

# A Visit to the Schoolhouse

Before we moved to Dutch Harbor, we had assumed that Becky would be homeschooled those three years. I had bought the Calvert Kindergarten course to get her started. Now that we were more familiar with the area and its facilities we began having second thoughts. We both felt Becky could benefit from a regular classroom experience plus the interaction with other children. We still had plenty of time before September to decide, since it was only January, but first we wanted to at least check out the school.

While I continued to teach Becky and Malcolm the Calvert's course at a regular time each day that winter in an effort to provide the structure that would accompany regular classes, Charlie and I discussed the future of the children's education. We knew we would eventually have to decide whether to continue homeschooling Becky in the fall for first grade or take advantage of the elementary school on Unalaska. It would present a great deal of inconvenience as Charlie would have to take Becky over in our skiff before he started work, which was not practical. If she were to attend I would probably have to rent an apartment and remain there during the weekdays, though financially that would not be easy trying to run two households on his paycheck. It would solve the weather problem, though, as there would be days when commuting would be impossible.

One afternoon Charlie took off work early so that we could go to Unalaska and visit the school. When we reached it the classes were just ending. The principal, Fred Kent, took us on a short tour. There were four teachers, four classrooms, and eight grades, with two classes to each room. The enrollment barely reached fifty. Fred taught the seventh and eighth grades as well as his administrative duties. He was about our age and it was his first year there so he was also fairly new to the community. Charlie and I hit it off with him right away as we discovered various things we had in common.

Fred introduced us to the first grade teacher, Cathy Slack, a cheerful outgoing lady, and she showed us around her room. We were impressed with what we saw. There seemed to be so much more to offer than what homeschooling would provide. There would be interaction with other students, competition, spelling bees, games – so many learning situations that come with group participation that my home schooling could not provide. But we still had the problem of either renting a place or finding a way to get Becky to school. We explained our problem to Fred and said we would have to think about it, we had plenty of time. He told us that the next time we came over he wanted to take us to meet his family.

The late winter months moved along at an uneventful pace as we spent some of our Saturdays at Unalaska shopping and visiting with people. During that time we met Fred Kent's family and spent some time with them. Since Charlie and I were former teachers we liked to rehash our old school days with Fred, which hadn't ended all that long ago for either of us. I learned that his wife, Jeanette, was an accomplished seamstress. One of my college minors had been Home Economics. I had taught both girls' and boys' Home Ec. at Seward and sewing happened to be one of my hobbies. I enjoyed making a lot of my clothes and Becky's. However, Jeanette was by far more skilled than I. She had the patience of a perfectionist that I lacked. Her's was more than a hobby.

Our new friendship also provided Malcolm with a male playmate, their son. Lowell was the same age and it didn't take long before they became very good friends. Eventually Lowell would have three younger

Malcolm and Becky Playing Dress-up

sisters, so he would be spared the indignity of an older sister playing dress-up with him.

Oh yes, I have not mentioned one of Becky's and Cookie's favorite games to play with Malcolm. They would go through Charlie's and my clothes and come up with some outlandish costumes, which included dressing Malcolm as if he were a giant doll. Because he was a good-natured child he went along with it and fit right in with their games. The clothes they picked were actually pretty close to costumes, considering the type of apparel we had with us when we arrived in those stormy islands.

*Chapter*

# 10

# Games Children Played

*The three* children loved the good weather days because they could play outside. I liked those days too but for different reasons; I could get more done in the house. Our house had a small terrace in front and when they found large empty pasteboard boxes - the kind toilet paper and large items came in - they opened up the bottoms, laid the boxes sideways end to end, and placed them along the top of the terrace. Then they crawled through them. Sometimes Charlie would come by when they were inside them and give the boxes a kick when they weren't expecting it, sending them rolling off the terrace inside the boxes, laughing and screeching all the way down to the dirt embankment just before the road. When there is no external entertainment, children seem to have a remarkable ability to create their own. But sometimes that got them into trouble.

One time Becky, Cookie and Malcolm found a coffee can full of nails in the shop and carried it out to the road. Cookie said, "Let's play 'parade' and this can be the confetti." Malcolm was too young to know about parades and had spent most of his short life in isolation but he always went along with whatever the girls wanted to do. So the three of them stood at the intersection between the shop and the two company homes on the gravel bank of the road and tossed handfuls of nails into it.

Just as they threw out some more nails Charlie drove by, then quickly brought his truck to a stop. "What the hell are you kids doing?" he yelled as he jumped out.

Innocently, Malcolm piped up, "We are throwing confetti at the parade."

'Pick up every damn one of them. Do you know what nails do to tires? They make holes in them and then I have to fix them. We don't have a store here to go buy new ones. And trucks can't run on flat tires." His angry voice made the three of them pick faster. They may not have understood everything he was telling them, but they did not need to. They were not used to such a reaction from Charlie. I was the disciplinarian, but on rare occasions when it was something serious he didn't hesitate to correct them.

He took Malcolm by the arm and gave him a couple of swats as he said, "And what were you doing in the shop anyway! I've told you to stay out of there. Go on in the house. Becky, give me that can. I'll put it back and you get on in the house, too. I think you better go home now, Cookie." While Malcolm didn't grasp the seriousness of nails in a road, the spanking left such an impression that years later he could still recall the incident.

On a lighter note, one of Malcolm's indoor favorite activities that directly involved Charlie was grabbing hold of the back pockets on his work coveralls after he got in the door from work. He would hold on and swing his feet off the floor so he could hang on while Charlie tried to walk. I scolded him and said I was getting tired of sewing up torn pockets. It seemed Charlie always had torn back pockets. But Malcolm was having too much fun. Charlie was good-natured about it but he knew I would be mad if he did not put an end to it. So one time he unzipped his suit when Malcolm came up behind him and grabbed the pockets and lifted up his feet, expecting a ride. The suit came down on top of him as he dropped to the floor. And that was the end of my concern about torn pockets.

Charlie wasn't above playing other pranks, too. When the fishermen came to the dock for fuel, Charlie often invited them up to our house to visit and they sometimes stayed for dinner. I enjoyed cooking so Charlie asked them fairly often. At one such dinner, the joke was on Becky. One

Becky and Malcolm, Empty Buildings in Background

of the guys had given him some fake (plastic) vomit and he hadn't showed it to any of us. With Becky sitting next to him at the table, he waited till she was looking away, and then placed it beside her plate. When she looked back, he exclaimed, "Look what you did!"

When she saw it she protested, "I didn't do that!" Then she took her napkin and tried to wipe it up. None of us could contain our laughter any longer. She became somewhat indignant, but not for long. She was 'Daddy's girl' and was used to his teasing.

Chapter

# 11

# Mama

By the first part of April we still had not made any decisions about Becky's schooling and had not said anything about it to our neighbors. They might not be too pleased if their daughter's playmates moved across the bay in the fall. We were not even sure that would happen, so why make waves? But when Sam Svarny at the RCA building in Unalaska notified me that I had a call on the radio from my dad in Overland Park, Kansas, I had a feeling it might be something serious because he had not called us since our move to the Aleutians the year before. I took the children across the street to stay with Cookie at the Beals' house and Charlie ran me across the bay in our skiff to take the call.

Because of the somewhat awkward means of communication, having to say 'over' before the other person could speak, Daddy just blurted out his news without any preliminaries. "Your mother was admitted to the hospital last night with severe abdominal pains. The x-rays showed a complete bowel obstruction. The doctor thinks it is cancer and is scheduling her for surgery right away. If you can be here Mother wants you with her. Over."

I was stunned. Mama, at age fifty-seven, had appeared in good health almost exactly a year ago when I last visited her before heading back to

Alaska. I had planned to put in a three year stint at Dutch Harbor before visiting again. My mother worked as a private duty nurse and had cared for many cancer patients, often terminal. I knew she was well aware of what awaited her if it were cancer, and the x-rays pointed in that direction. And I wanted to be with her. I did not hesitate or even ask Charlie. Schooling plans for Becky went on hold.

"I will try and get out on the next flight, Daddy. There's a plane due in tomorrow. I can call you from Anchorage so that you will know when the children and I will arrive. Tell Mama I will be there. Over."

When I ended the conversation, I turned to Charlie and told him that I needed to go to my parents' home as soon as possible. He said he understood and would notify Reeve Aleutian Airways when we got back on the other side. Sam said he was sorry to hear about my mother and would also let Gert know I would be gone for a while.

When I got back home I explained to Becky and Malcolm that Grandma was sick so we were going to go visit her. They seemed excited about the prospect of travelling. No mention was made of their miserable flight the previous year. Apparently, young children can sometimes forget traumatic situations rather quickly. We were on the next plane out of there.

The DC-3 flight was a bit rough and bouncy again, though it was nothing like that initial ride. We got off at Cold Bay where we only had a short wait to change planes to the DC-6, which would take us to Anchorage. This gave me time to clean up Malcolm -- again. He had not developed his 'flight stomach' yet. I felt a little 'green' myself, but Becky was holding her own – no pun intended. But the rest of our trip to Anchorage and then on to Kansas City in a large jet was uneventful, meaning no one threw up.

Mama's surgery was scheduled for the day after I got there; I had made it just in time. I had received my nurses' training from that hospital and one of my favorite specialties had been the operating room, and I had worked for a while in New Mexico as an operating room nurse afterward. The surgeon allowed me to remain in the OR with Mama as she had requested. She seemed calm and accepting about what would be happening, though she was fairly certain what they would find. She seemed to take comfort in my hand on her arm as she looked up at me when she was wheeled into the OR, where I was given a cap, gown and mask to wear. After the anesthetic was started, I stood to one side, out of the way.

Once the initial incision was made, a pathologist's report was not necessary to validate the obvious findings. The doctor estimated she might have one or two more years. Mama's attitude was good and when she was given the sad news, she made it clear that she was determined to live as long as she could. Even though it was major surgery she didn't remain in the hospital long. She wanted to be in her own home and get on with the remainder of her life as well as she still could under these changed circumstances. While she no longer worked, she was able to visit her friends quite often, something she enjoyed, as she was a sociable, outgoing person. She also liked to sew so she even started new projects.

My sister, Mary, and her large family – seven children at that time- lived next door so they visited Mama every day and helped when they could. When Mama seemed comfortable with her condition, and with my sister next door, I decided to head back to Dutch Harbor. But I let Daddy know that I was willing –and wanted – to come back and help with Mama later on in the future when I suspected I would be needed.

Although we had been gone for only a little over a month, spring had come to the Aleutians and the weather had more good days than bad. Our return trip thankfully was uneventful, and when I spotted the familiar site of Mt Ballyhoo from the window of the DC-3 as we approached Dutch Harbor, I had the happy feeling that I was returning home.

Chapter

# 12

# Fourth of July Race

*Shortly after* getting resettled in our house, I started my greenhouse plants, mostly vegetables, as they provided our best source of fresh produce. I was getting a late start but they would be a welcome addition to our diet when they did show up. What was available in the stores and from boats was very expensive and not always fresh.

I resumed the Calvert kindergarten classes for Becky, Cookie, and Malcolm right away. Because of the interruption, I extended the class time so we could cover more material; I wanted Becky to have a 'head start' for first grade in the fall which was just a few months away. The material may have seemed a little advanced for Cookie and Malcolm, but they were very quick learners and enthusiastic students.

Perhaps because we were busy with the course material, the children and I looked forward to the approaching holiday, the Fourth of July, for a welcome break from our routine. We made plans to go over to Unalaska for their annual festivities as the town always had special events planned and made a real celebration of the holiday.

One event that both Becky and Malcolm enjoyed was the races. From toddlers to adults, there were races for all to participate. They were held on a large field between the beach and the storefronts where there was plenty of room for everyone to congregate. All the village children would be competing with their own age group, just running from one end to the other, and not a very long stretch. Each winner would be given a can of pop. The adults were more creative, and their three-legged races and gunny sack races had everybody laughing.

Malcolm was a lightweight with no baby fat, not like some chubby two and three year olds. He liked to run and was surprisingly fast for his size. While he was almost three, alongside the other boys and girls, he was the smallest in his group. That didn't concern me; young as he was, he had already shown a desire to be the best at whatever he attempted.

I was not sure if Malcolm knew about the can of pop prize or if he was that interested in it. But he liked candy. When we lined up our children, I whispered to Malcolm, "I'll give you a piece of candy when you get to the other side." He could relate to that. When the toddlers were told to run to the finish line where their parents waited, the mothers tried to encourage them. They would yell, "Run! Run! Get pop!" The shouts fell on deaf ears with some of them as they just walked around. But Malcolm streaked across the lawn in front of all the others and ran straight to me, his first words, "Where's my candy?" Of course, I rewarded him.

Actually, his win was not a fluke. He liked running and as he grew older became a very fast runner. Then in his teens he became a local hockey star for his tremendous speed on ice.

Becky was another story. She raced with her age group, the five year olds, but was not as enthusiastic about running or getting a can of pop, and couldn't be bribed with a piece of candy. She raced simply for the fun of being with the kids she had befriended on our trips to Unalaska. She enjoyed the race in her own way.

That same afternoon Fred and Jeanette and their children were also there. Fred said he'd like to talk to me later. So when the festivities were over, our family went to their place. Fred told me that there was a teaching position available as one of the teachers had decided not to return in the fall. I had mentioned earlier that I was a licensed teacher for both elementary and secondary classes. He asked if I would be interested in applying as he'd

Unalaska Children's Races, Becky in Blue Jacket on Left

have to get someone lined up soon. I hadn't given any thought to working since we lived on a separate island, plus Malcolm was not quite three.

"I really do appreciate the offer. I'll think about it. Charlie and I haven't decided yet about Becky's schooling. We'll have a lot of things to work out if I take the position, though I like the idea of Becky being in a regular classroom and around other children. However, we haven't totally given up on our original homeschooling idea. I know you are running out of time so I will get back to you in a day or two one way or the other."

After we returned to Dutch Harbor later that day, we didn't say much about Fred's offer as we were pretty tired, having been gone most of the day. But the more I thought about it, my taking that position would solve several problems. If we rented one of Pops' kitchenettes we could stay in the village. That would solve the transportation problem. I would get a babysitter for Malcolm and could pay for that and the rent with my salary. I just had to sell Charlie on the idea. He had not acted too happy about it when Fred had brought it up and didn't really show signs of wanting to discuss it. I knew he was leaning toward our being home seven days a week instead of two, for different reasons. He liked being with his kids and me and our day-to-day family life. This would change that. I didn't blame him but I knew he would still be going through his busy season for a while in the fall, and maybe not even notice that we were not there.

I did have a misgiving of my own, though. I was not sure that I was ready to turn Malcolm over to a babysitter five days a week. Also, I knew that I would miss our home life routine. I had become spoiled. I had worked most of my married life, and after finding out what it was like to be a homemaker and a stay-at home mom, I was reluctant to give that up.

For the next two days, I made sure we talked about the situation quite a bit when Charlie was home, as I knew I had to give Fred Kent an answer soon or it would be a moot point. Charlie and I finally agreed that my taking the job was the best solution for Becky.

He said, "I'll ask Walter if he knows of someone whom he can trust and be reliable that could take care of Malcolm during school hours." Charlie liked working with Walter and relied on his judgement.

I sent word to Fred and let him know I would take the position and would be over as soon as Charlie had enough time off to take me so I could fill out the necessary papers, and I'd rent a place while there.

When Walter got back to us he said his good friend, Mrs. Moller, agreed to take care of Malcolm. I already knew her. She had a kind and gentle nature and I liked her very much. She would have been my first choice. I just hadn't known if she'd do it. She had watched him and Becky before when Charlie and I went to Unalaska for an occasional community dance. He seemed to enjoy being there.

Everything was falling into place, but I still had to tell our neighbors. Their reaction was just what I had feared. They were unhappy that the children and I would be staying at Unalaska five days a week, that Cookie would not have a playmate during that time, nor would I be teaching her. I felt bad that Becky wouldn't be with her constant companion of over a year, but I assured the neighbors that we would be back on weekends whenever possible. I could sympathize with them, and especially with their little daughter, as I knew it would upset their routine, but I had my own problems to deal with - the disruption in our family, trying to live between two islands and my mother's illness. Life has a way of changing one's plans.

## Chapter 13

# Unalaska and Anfesia

That September of 1962 Becky, Malcolm, and I settled into our one room kitchenette at Unalaska. After taking Malcolm to Mrs. Moller's, Becky and I walked to the schoolhouse from there, about the equivalent of a long block on gravel roads. The school itself was a simple one-story rectangular frame building. Besides a gymnasium there were four classrooms with two grades in each one. I was assigned the third and fourth grades with six pupils in each. I really enjoyed my twelve students; they were fun to be with and they enjoyed being there, perhaps partly because of the isolation of the island. They showed it with their enthusiasm. Mrs. Moller's youngest child, Sandra, was one of my fourth graders. During school hours it felt like she and I just exchanged children. Because this was the smallest group I had ever worked with, we were able to make great progress with lots of individual attention.

There are some obvious advantages to these small remote schools. By comparison, the year I taught in Seward I had fifty-four students in ninth grade English alone divided into two classes, plus three other classes on other subjects. As time went on Charlie and I knew we had made the right decision. Becky was provided with a classroom full of children her own age and all the learning facilities available. Malcolm seemed to be faring all right, too. Mrs. Moller had grandchildren she took care of sometimes and they were not all girls, plus they were closer to his age. When he told me he had fun playing with them I knew it was also a good move for him.

When the weather was good and Charlie was not working he picked us up on Friday afternoon and took us back home. I got caught up on the laundry and housecleaning and prepared some food ahead for Charlie. So far our arrangement seemed to be working out. However, there were weekends when the bay was too rough for the children and me to go across, but often Charlie would come over anyway and stay with us. He had stronger nerves than I did when it came to rough water and he enjoyed having the time to go visiting. He wasn't really happy that we were away so much but he knew it was best.

One of the people we had become friends with was Anfesia Shapsnikoff, said by others to be one of the best Aleut grass basket weavers. We were told that her baskets were as fine and delicate as cloth. When Charlie and I paid her a visit, she showed us several small baskets that were both flawlessly made and beautiful. She explained the slow tedious process of preparing the raw materials and the skill required to turn the grass into objects of utilitarian art. After we had purchased one on that first visit, she offered us tea. She was quite a sociable lady and told us a lot of interesting and enjoyable stories about our new home and about her life. I felt I had been given a first-hand glimpse of local history and the feelings of wanting to be a part of that place grew stronger. Later, Charlie told me that he shared the same thoughts.

Anfesia was tiny and at first appeared elderly and frail. Then she began to speak and it was immediately apparent that she was neither frail nor elderly or the least bit helpless. She was only in her sixties and exhibited boundless energy, plus she was well-versed in many things, not just her exceptional talent for basket-weaving. That day she became one of our growing list of friends.

While sitting in her living room that day I noticed lying on a chair a half-finished knitting project. When I commented on it she showed me a really nice sweater that she'd almost finished. After that visit, Charlie and I made it a point to stop and see her often. Sometimes her son, Phil Tutiakoff, was there, also, as friendly and outgoing as his mother. Phil was a lively conversationalist, expressing strong opinions about a variety of subjects. One he seemed to feel quite seriously about was Native Rights, a popular topic in those days with statehood having just been granted several years before.

It was after one of these visits that I stopped by after school and asked Anfesia if I could hire her to knit Charlie a sweater/jacket as I would like to give him one for a Christmas present. When she agreed I ordered the pattern and materials and took them to her. She told me it would be ready in time for Christmas.

By December I knew I was pregnant again. Charlie and I had both hoped for a large family so we were excited about the prospect of another child. The loss of the pregnancy in the summer of '61 still troubled us but we felt another baby would help us move on. I didn't think that being pregnant would interfere with my teaching job as I wasn't due till after the school year ended, not till July. I don't think the school board would have forced me to resign if they knew, but I decided to keep quiet about it for as long as I could, except for alerting Fred Kent about my condition.

I was more concerned with the possibility that I would need to make an unscheduled trip to Overland Park. But the word I kept receiving from my family back there was that Mama was doing well, considering her prognosis. She would still go shopping and visiting with my dad or sister, and was not having much discomfort. I hoped to get through the school year, and then go back out after I had my baby.

Chapter

# 14

# Christmas of '62

In early December, Fred called a teachers' meeting, which meant the other two teachers and me. "We have to put on a Christmas program for the school. This is my first year as principal so I'm unfamiliar with that program. I want each of you to decide what your room will do and we'll get something put together. "

I already had my own ideas. I had previously done a little playwriting so I told Fred, "No problem. I would like my class to put on a short play. I've actually been thinking about one that has a Nativity scene, you know, with shepherds and wise men. What about that?"

He smiled, but I detected a little sarcasm. "How original. Fine with me. I still have to come up with something for my class, though." As principal, plus teaching two classes, he didn't have as much extra time as I did.

In our small community all of the school productions were considered big events and attended by most of the village. Because I had been an English major and had also taken playwriting, I tried to relieve some of the pressure. "I can help as much as you need, Fred. I enjoy putting on programs." As it turned out, the other two teachers, who were familiar with such grade school productions, had also been making a few plans of their own.

I wrote the play, and the class devised costumes for their roles, maybe kind of hokey by bigger schools' standards but we worked with what we had and I think that gave it more of a 'children's production' look. Becky was a sheep for the first grade class part of the program. I glued gobs of cotton on one of Charlie's old jackets after turning it inside out so that the white lining showed between the cotton balls. She looked like a first grader in sheep's clothing. I think the audience got the idea.

I thought back to the previous Christmas when our family had come over to see a school Christmas program and we had seen those lights from a big ship anchored off in the bay. Time seemed to be going by much faster than we had hoped. Charlie had only a little over a year left on Dutch Harbor before the company would transfer him to who knew where. We did not talk much about it but we were hoping to find a way to extend our stay.

Before our Christmas break, I visited Anfesia and she had Charlie's sweater/jacket ready, just as she had promised. The color of the wool was off white with a wolf design on the back and a few evergreen trees – very Alaskan looking and beautiful. When I gave it to Charlie it was a good fit though it was the first time he had put it on. He only wore it for nonworking occasions so as not to get it soiled, but he had the use of it for many years. When people asked him who made it, he would tell them about the tiny remarkable lady who had done such fine work.

During the Christmas vacation Becky, Malcolm and I went back to our home at Dutch Harbor for a few weeks. I again told my parents that I was going to have another baby, due in July. I also notified my Anchorage doctor. Though it wasn't due till school ended, Fred Kent told me that if for any reason I could not continue he would put a substitute in for me. There were several people in the village that he could call on as there had been a few times when one of the teachers had been ill and he had used them as subs. I felt a little better knowing that, thinking about Mama being a reason I might have to leave early.

That December Charlie told me that the huge sheep ranch at Chernofski on the other end of Unalaska Island was butchering older sheep and taking orders for mutton. He suggested we order one, too, as the price was very reasonable. I agreed that it would be good to have our freezer full of meat.

Charlie developed a working relationship with Milt Holmes, the rancher who was in charge. Charlie also agreed to contact people in the village and take orders whenever Milt was getting ready to butcher, then when the carcasses arrived Charlie would deliver them and collect the money for Milt.

I do not know if that was the start of Charlie's interest in sheep, but about that time he started talking about leasing some island grazing land that the Bureau of Land Management had available. Neither of us wanted to leave the Aleutians and he may have thought that was a way we could remain on the Chain. It was more than I had been able to come up with. I had considered continuing my teaching contract if he quit Standard Oil, but then he would have to find work. So maybe ranching, working for ourselves, had some possibilities for us. He was born on and grew up on his father's Hereford cattle ranch in the mountains of New Mexico, though sheep ranching isn't quite the same.

By the time I returned to my classroom in January, 1963, Charlie seemed more serious about homesteading and starting a sheep ranch, since that was mainly what he talked about. He apparently had been looking into it quite a bit during my absence while teaching. I am an adventurous person by nature so I had no serious misgivings about the idea, partly because it was just an idea. We did not even know how much it would take. So that January it was just a dream, mostly Charlie's, and I didn't take it very seriously.

Chapter

# 15

# Back in Kansas

*The news* I had been dreading came right after the Christmas break on the marine radio in Unalaska. I had only been back in the classroom a few weeks when Sam Svarny sent a message to the school that I had a call from Kansas. I had been expecting it. I had just hoped it would come later.

"Mother had to go back in the hospital for more surgery. Would you be able to come again, at least for a little while? I could use some help. Over." Daddy's voice sounded tired and sad.

Of course I would, but I knew what I had to do first. I had my class, so I told Daddy that I would talk it over with the principal and explain the situation. As soon as he could get a replacement I would be there to help him with Mama. I knew it was hard on Daddy as he still had to keep working five evenings a week at his assembly line job at the General Motors plant. The medical bills kept piling up and the insurance only covered part of it. Though my sister Mary lived right next door, her seven children were still very young. She had her hands full between them and helping Daddy with Mama. I felt somewhat selfish in my more comfortable position, plus I was a trained nurse and could be of greater help in caring for Mama.

Right after the phone call I notified Charlie then went to see Fred Kent to give him the news. He was able to get an older woman who was staying in Unalaska with her daughter who happened to be the fifth and sixth grade teacher. She was somewhat familiar with my classes as she substituted for me once when I missed a day with morning sickness. At the time, Fred had wondered aloud if I would make it through the school year, but I assured him I would be fine, that I hardly ever got morning sickness. And this baby was not due till after school ended. Now here I was leaving for a totally different reason. I could not know when I would be back so I did not expect Fred to hold the job for me. I let Mrs. Moller know and Pops, then started packing up our things at the apartment. When Charlie came to get us after he got off work he said he notified Reeve Aleutian that there would be three passengers on their next flight out of Dutch Harbor. He would go back to the apartment after we left and finish closing it up. I felt bad about having to leave him again but we both knew it was inevitable.

When we arrived back at Overland Park, Kansas, Mama was still in the hospital in Kansas City. Overland Park is only about twenty miles from there, not an inconvenient distance. Daddy took me right in to see her and she seemed in good spirits, though the doctor had done more surgery. She sounded reconciled to her condition but didn't like being in the hospital. She wanted to be in her own home surrounded by family and her own familiar things. Now that I was there and could administer her shots and other meds, she was able to talk the doctor into letting her go back home to Overland Park. That would also make it easier for Daddy and my sister to get to be with her more.

Once we were settled, I enrolled Becky in the first grade at a private Catholic school so that she would not miss any schooling. Shortly afterward, however, she became unwilling to leave the house to go to the school bus stop with her cousins. That was not her usual nature. Without telling me what was wrong, she just refused to go with them and said she wanted to stay home. I would sometimes have to drive her there pretty much against her will. She had always liked school, and she liked being with her cousins. But she would not tell me what was wrong. Of course, this couldn't keep up, so eventually, I got to the root of Becky's resistance. She told me that the teacher, a lay teacher not a nun, had slapped her because she wrote her name in pencil in one of her books. This was back in the days when a teacher could get away with such behavior. Had Becky told me when it had happened I would have gone to that school immediately and reported the incident to the principal. But it was some time later, so with the time lapse, all I really wanted was to get Becky out of that school and back to Dutch Harbor. But first I had to be sure others could take over giving Mama her shots.

A student nurse that was a friend of Mama's lived near our home and sometimes stopped in to see her. As Mama got to feeling a little better and was able to be up and around again she asked her friend if she would give her the meds and shots that I had been administering. The girl agreed, so I got our plane tickets to get back to Alaska and Dutch Harbor. We had been gone about two months. One more time I bid my parents good-by, knowing in my heart another call in the future was inevitable. Mama had already used up a year of her estimated remaining time. But I hoped to have completed my pregnancy and have my new baby before I would get that call.

Becky was especially happy to be leaving and of course Charlie was glad to get the news of our return, saying he did not like his bachelor life, and he also missed the kids very much. While I was waiting in Anchorage for the Reeve Aleutian plane I saw my doctor for a final check-up. He said since the baby wasn't due until late July, I did not need to return till about the middle of that month. We then headed back to Dutch Harbor, fortunately an uneventful trip, though I made sure to check the pockets in front of all three seats and got out the barf bags. Experience paid off.

## Chapter 16

# A Ranch?

After we had resettled in Dutch Harbor, Charlie reminded me that there was less than a year remaining on his contract and Standard Oil was thinking of transferring him to Anchorage. While Dutch Harbor had its challenges, with a new baby on the way we still did not want to leave the island. We saw only the benefits of our new life, its natural beauty and exciting weather patterns, the warmth of the people, the simple life, and a safe place to raise children. What was there not to like? Of course, there were advantages to cities but we didn't have to live in them, just travel there as needed.

One evening Charlie wanted to have a serious talk about our situation. "We're running out of time. If we want to stay here, we have to come up with a plan. I've been thinking a lot about leasing some BLM land under the Homestead Act. But that requires more money than we have in savings. There are lease rental fees, plus we would have to come up with a formal plan of how the land would be developed. For instance, what would be the land use, raise sheep or other farm animals, or grow something? I'm still leaning toward sheep since they have really thrived over on Chernofski and on Umnak, though I don't know much about raising them."

Should that be a red flag? If it was I wouldn't have cared. It was beginning to sound like a plan. And I actually liked the sound of it.

Charlie continued, "My dad's ranch just had cattle, Herefords. While you were gone, I communicated with Milt a few times and got some tips on raising sheep. I think I could do it. He sounded very helpful and said I could call on him anytime."

Charlie seemed so enthusiastic I did not want to play devil's advocate. I saw no point in talking him out of the idea when I couldn't come up with some other plan to help us remain in the Chain. Plus I thought homesteading and ranching in this unique setting sounded like a great adventure, risky as it was. That is just who I am. I have always been willing to take chances. But money was our biggest problem. If this was going to happen, it would take us at least a few more years to save up enough.

That spring Charlie contacted his boss in Anchorage and requested an extension of another year, which would give us more time to save money since it cost us so little to live at Dutch Harbor. Our housing and utilities were provided and the groceries were inexpensive since we ordered case lots out of Seattle. They were shipped at no charge by various boats coming up from Seattle, so we were able to save most of Charlie's paycheck.

At first, the response from Standard Oil to Charlie's request was guarded. They seemed to have an aversion to leaving employees in isolated areas too long, perhaps concerned that they might develop mental problems. But it did not take three years - more like three months - for Charlie and me to decide we wanted to make our home in the Aleutians. Finally word came that Standard Oil had agreed on another year, but they made it very clear there would be no more extensions. We now had a little over a year to come up with a plan to remain in the Aleutians. That did not seem like enough time, considering that all of the ideas we came up with involved more money than we had, but we were grateful for the extension. Knowing it would be our last year on Dutch Harbor we would try to enjoy as much as possible the time we had left.

But for the time being, we concentrated our thoughts on the new baby, making the necessary preparations to have everything ready. We anticipated there would be some definite changes in our household. I tried to prepare

Becky and Malcolm for the new addition. They asked a few questions but hadn't quite grasped the reality of a baby living with them. I also made arrangements to be gone for a few weeks. Friends in Anchorage had said I could stay with them while waiting to go into labor so I planned to remain in Dutch Harbor as close to the expected date as possible and just hoped I would not cut it too close.

The manager's wife agreed to have Becky and Malcolm stay at her house while Charlie was at work, an arrangement that Becky, Malcolm and Cookie looked forward to. It was the busiest time of year for Charlie with tankers, tugboats and barges filling the bay, along with the fishing boats. He was often down at the fuel dock for eighteen to twenty hours at a stretch without coming home, either offloading tankers out of California or pumping thousands of gallons of fuel into barges. He would just take his meals on one of the boats. Although it was an exhausting time for him he fell into the routine.

Becky and Malcolm grew more excited about getting a new brother or sister since we had first talked about it. Baby clothes that I had ordered from the Sears catalog arrived in the mail, so tiny they looked like doll clothes, and I packed them in what I called my 'maternity suitcase'. Charlie and I talked about names and we settled on Glen Allen if it was a boy, and Patricia if a girl. I don't know why, we both just liked those names.

Charlie and I had been married eight years and had only two children to show for it. We had hoped for a large family. Charlie was one of ten, I was one of four, and all our siblings had close relationships with each other. Already I wondered if our two children might not share that same closeness, with so many years between them. Before we were sent out to Dutch Harbor we had gone to two specialists to be tested. Both doctors informed us that there was nothing wrong, that there were various reasons why some women were unable to conceive as often as others. It would happen in its own good time, just be patient, they said. I was not known for my patience, but I found myself in a situation over which I had no control. I was forced to learn patience. Now here I was with a little one just under the surface, kicking me occasionally just to remind me that it was there.

One afternoon Charlie came in the house and said, "Look out the window at what's at the dock." All we could see what appeared to be a small black object on the outside of the railing, too close to the dock to make it out. "Get in the truck and I'll take you down there."

I assumed it was something special or he wouldn't have come home in the middle of the day to get us. The children pestered Charlie as to what it could be, but he mysteriously just kept saying, "You will see," as he headed for the dock. I had no idea what it was, but I could tell he wanted it to be a surprise, so I kept quiet, though I really wanted to know, too.

When we arrived at the dock he took us to the outer railing and we saw that it was a submarine! The reason we hadn't been able to see it before was because it was low tide. Since, the children and I had never seen a submarine it was indeed a surprising site. But the special treat was not over.

We were invited on board for a tour, first having to descend down a long ladder from the dock to the somewhat curved surface, where men in uniform were standing around. We were then taken down below, again another ladder, and shown some compartments which were equipped with heavy metal doors designed to shut water-tight. The sub looked pretty much like what I had seen in the movies, but I never dreamed I would find myself inside of one. I am no more claustrophobic than the average person, but once inside I knew it must take a certain kind of person to endure the limitations of such confinement. However, as a lay person I was fascinated by the experience and Becky and Malcolm were also impressed by what they saw. I chalked up one more 'first', an event I would never have experienced had I remained in Kansas.

Chapter

# 17

# Angel of Mercy

*July 17, 1963*, was a plane day. The sky was clear and the DC-3 had made it to Nikolski, the next village over, where it overnighted before its return trip to Cold Bay via Dutch Harbor. Earlier that morning I had awakened Charlie after I was certain the discomfort I felt coming from my back and moving toward my abdomen was not just the usual result of my advanced pregnancy – I had already experienced plenty of that. No, it had gone from an occasional cramp to a regular pattern of increasing intensity with measureable time between contractions. I no longer doubted what was happening – I recognized that feeling – labor pains. It is not predictable when they might start. Due dates are approximate.

I had already informed our Anchorage friends that I planned to fly there the following week and wait out the commencement of labor. I just did not want to be away from my family for very long. I had assumed the hospital would not release a newborn to a fairly remote island for at least a few days, so I anticipated having to wait at least a week before taking my new baby home.

Some women in the Unalaska village had their babies at home with the help of several local midwives. Others decided to go to the Native hospital in Anchorage, ANS, prior to labor and enjoy the comfort and safety of well-equipped delivery rooms, nurseries and trained doctors. Childbirth is a natural experience but in an effort to cut down on maternal and infant mortality more women were opting for hospital deliveries whenever possible. However, on that July morning I found myself in the early stages of labor on an isolated, sparsely populated island in the North Pacific, eight hundred air miles from the Anchorage hospital.

Charlie jumped out of bed and called Sam Svarny on our primitive phone system that was connected to only three other houses out there. Sam would get someone in Unalaska to send one of the midwives to Dutch Harbor as fast as possible. Charlie then headed to the airstrip to alert Larry Shaishnikoff, the airport attendant who came over from Unalaska to meet every plane and handle communications with Reeve Aleutian. He told Larry I would be on the plane to Cold Bay. It was still early so the plane wasn't due in yet.

Then Charlie went around to the boat landing and picked up not one, but two midwives, Anfesia Shapsnikoff and Mary Robinson. Since I was already friends with both of the women, I was glad they were the ones who came - and I couldn't have hoped for better midwives. Their presence and comforting words relieved some of my stress. When they met with me and assessed the situation, they both felt I should make it to Cold Bay as that was usually around an hour's flight, but neither wanted to speculate about the much longer flight to Anchorage.

That prompted Charlie to get on the marine radio in his office next to the kitchen and start trying to make contact with the Navy at Kodiak, requesting they send a plane with a doctor to meet the DC-3 in Cold Bay and transport me to the Kodiak hospital. The Navy was always willing to meet the various emergencies, so it was reassuring to us that they would be involved in my transport.

Everything seemed to be happening very fast, though I was oblivious to a lot of the activity around me as my contractions increased in intensity. Mary tried to reassure me as she helped me to dress and prepare for the journey. She told me that she gave birth to her twelfth baby in December of the previous year, a little girl she named Piama, and the delivery did not have any complications. I sometimes stopped at Verne's grocery store in Unalaska, to buy some fresh produce and visit with her. She was always friendly and made me feel comfortable with her. Her daughter, Marcia, was one of my third graders when I taught school the previous fall. She looked a lot like her mother, very pretty, with long black hair and bangs, the way Mary sometimes wore hers. She had the sweet friendly smile I always associated with Mary.

As Anfesia tried to distract me from my increasing discomfort she told me how she had given birth to twins many years ago, then placed them in a grass basket she had made and covered them with moss to keep them warm. She said I should do just fine with all the modern help. She spoke with such confidence while holding my hand that I was able to relax a little and keep my moaning to a minimum.

I heard the Reeve Aleutian plane just as Charlie came in the room and took my 'maternity suitcase' and said we needed to get going. Then he turned to the two women and asked, "Which one of you is going with Joan?"

Mary and Anfesia looked at each other in surprise. Neither had brought personal belongings with them. No one had mentioned the possibility of traveling with me, but I could understand that it made sense and I would feel less stressed if I had someone with me.

Charlie told the midwives, "The crew said there must be a midwife on board or they are not going to take her." I knew they did not want an inflight delivery without a midwife; neither did I.

Though Mary and I were friends I had not considered her a close friend, but she did not hesitate as she responded calmly, "I will go with her. The older girls can take care of things, and Verne's there."

Gratefully, I said, "Thank you, Mary." I knew I could not have gotten on that plane without her – and I didn't want to. Now if I could just be quiet so that the crew would not refuse to let me board, as it was getting harder and harder to be silent as the pain increased.

Fortunately, I was able to mask any moans so they let me on, since I had a midwife with me and it was not a long flight. Upon boarding I was in too much discomfort to sit in a seat so I asked the stewardess if she had

Mary Robinson (Turnpaugh) and Joan, 49 Years Later

something she could put down so that I could lie on the cabin floor. There were few passengers so there was plenty of space. She placed a thin unpadded canvas stretcher on the hard floor, and Mary helped me to lie down. Then the stewardess handed her a blanket to cover me. Mary knelt next to me instead of taking a seat, and held my hand all the way to Cold Bay, trying to comfort me with soft gentle words.

As the contractions became excruciatingly painful I could not suppress the loud moans which I'm sure must have frightened the few passengers and the stewardess. Maybe they were worried that they might have to be involved in a delivery; I would not blame them! The cockpit door was open so the pilot and co-pilot probably heard me over the drone of the engines. Later, the pilot told me it was the fastest trip he had ever made between Dutch Harbor and Cold Bay.

After the plane landed, with Mary walking by my side I was carried on the canvas stretcher to a first-aid station near the airport to await the arrival of the Navy plane, the Albatross. By then I was in a great deal of discomfort - actually pain, with no drugs to alleviate the increasing intensity. Again I was placed on the floor, this time cold gray concrete directly under the thin canvas stretcher. In spite of my advancing labor, I was able to make out an examining table in the small room. Why I was placed on the hard floor puzzled me, but I had no time to protest. The two stretcher-bearers had quickly laid me down then disappeared out the door and closed it behind them. Again Mary knelt by me and held my hand and spoke in comforting tones. It became impossible for me to 'suffer in silence' as the contractions became more severe. I could hear voices outside the door, but no one opened it to check on me or offer Mary anything, though it was about an hour before the Navy plane arrived. I didn't fault them as I was unprepared for natural childbirth and was making such frightening sounds that they were not encouraged to enter.

At some point I felt very nauseated, though I hadn't eaten anything since I woke early that morning with labor contractions. I suddenly told Mary, "I'm going to throw up!" a not uncommon occurrence in late stages of labor. As Mary continued to kneel by my side, she helped me to raise my head. Not seeing a receptacle in the near vicinity she cupped her hands to form a bowl and placed them under my chin so that when I vomited it would not go on me or the floor. Then she went to the sink and washed her hands. I had never before had anyone perform such a selfless act of kindness for me, and at that point she was not even a close friend. From the time Mary reached my bedside in Dutch Harbor I never saw anyone offer her food or drink till we reached Kodiak, though she never left my side and never complained about her own discomfort. Such simple behavior was profound in its selflessness.

Cold Bay – Cross Made by Fred Barnett, Fire Chief

# Chapter 18

# Delivery

About an hour after our arrival the door to the first aid room burst open and a tall young man wearing a khaki military uniform entered the room, followed by another serviceman pushing an incubator. I saw a couple of other people also enter that I assumed were some of the FAA employees. The young man introduced himself as the Navy doctor. His first command was to have two of the FAA men lift me onto the padded examining table. He may have been as puzzled as I was as to why I had been put on the floor. After I was placed on the table he examined me, and then stated that my labor was too advanced to move me, that the delivery was imminent; it was going to happen in that first-aid room, and soon.

As he arranged things and slipped on sterile gloves amidst my cries, he explained they couldn't give me any pain medication and reassured me that it would soon be over, just a few more good contractions. Again Mary positioned herself at my side and held my hand, though more correctly I dug my fingers into her hand. I let out a final cry of pain accompanied by that last unstoppable push, followed by abrupt silence; the doctor had been there about twenty minutes. Prior to the sudden stillness he had been offering me soft words of encouragement, and then it was over.

After a few moments had gone by, he looked up at me and asked, "What religion are you?" and I knew my baby was dead.

Stunned, I replied, "Catholic," as I tried to comprehend what had just happened.

I had worked as an RN in various Catholic hospitals before I moved to Alaska and I had delivered over seventy babies unassisted. I knew it was standard procedure to immediately baptize stillborn infants.

"I'm Episcopalian," he told me. "Would you like me to baptize the baby or have someone else do it?"

His previous question had prepared me. I was no longer moaning loudly. I had little energy even to cry. Exhausted, I said, "I would like you to do it. Is my baby a boy or a girl?"

"It's a boy. Do you have a name picked out?" He still hadn't told me the baby was dead; he may have been reluctant to say the words.

"Glen Allen. If it was a boy that is the name my husband and I had picked." I was still very subdued, perhaps a bit in shock from the recent events. Mary had let go of my hand and stepped back but she continued to stand near me. In this room of heartbreak surrounded by strangers, her presence seemed to have a comforting effect.

As he performed the brief baptismal ceremony, I turned my head and watched the technician wheel the empty incubator out of the aid station, a symbolic end to the past few hours, and the past nine months. I watched helplessly as the doctor handed a small bundle enclosed in a blanket to a gray-haired middle-age man who had approached the table. They did not exchange words, though I noted the man appeared to have a solemn expression.

"Couldn't I see the baby?" I asked the doctor, just above a whisper, as the man carried the wrapped infant out the door.

In a gentle voice he said, "You have your own memory of him. It is better to remember him that way." I knew he was right, though it wasn't what I had wanted to hear. In time, I would appreciate his thoughtfulness.

But I had more questions. "Why did he die? How long was he dead?"

"We don't really know why some babies die after they have made it through nine months, but sometimes labor can be very traumatic for them. He had probably been dead no more than eight hours, since he wasn't macerated."

"What does that mean?"

"It refers to the stage of decomposition of a stillborn that starts after about that time." He spoke softly in the somber atmosphere.

I turned toward Mary. I was still holding it together. I had been through this before. Now it had happened again – I had been so close. Would we ever have more children? I didn't know if I could handle another disappointment. "Please, could someone call Charlie and let him know?" I dreaded to ask, not wanting him to hear the unexpected news, knowing that call would cause a similar pain of loss, but he needed to know as soon as possible.

"I'll ask someone here at the airport to call him and let him know," Mary said, still standing near me. "Also, I'll have them tell Charlie that I'm going with you to Kodiak, and to let Verne know. But we shouldn't be gone more than a week or two."

"Thanks, Mary, and thank you for everything." I had not seen her eat or drink anything since we were at my house that morning. I hoped she had eaten before she got the call to go over to Dutch. She had to be feeling weak from such an ordeal, yet she never sat down, just stayed by my side on the plane's wood floor, then on the concrete floor of the emergency station.

Then I closed my eyes as the reality of the situation sank in. My tears came soundlessly, unlike my noisy hysterical sobs two years before. Resignation had taken over.

I was placed back on the stretcher and two men carried me out the door toward the Navy plane that would transport me to the Kodiak hospital. As we went across the tarmac a man not in a military uniform approached my side. I recognized him as the one who had carried the little bundle out.

"I'm the Cold Bay Fire Chief," he said as I looked up at him. "I am going to make a little coffin and a cross marker and bury your baby on a hillside outside of Cold Bay. There is one other grave there. A Russian woman died on a boat in the early nineteen hundreds and is buried there. It is a very nice spot."

I thanked him for his kindness. I was comforted by his thoughtfulness. In my grief of the moment it did not quite register with me all that he told me at the time. He had probably been one of those standing on the other side of the aid station door that I had scared half to death with my loud cries. And yet he had found a way to ease my pain.

Chapter

# 19

## Kodiak

*The flight* to Kodiak was a study in contrasts. When Mary and I made the trip to Cold Bay I lay on a sheet of canvas covering the wood floor, while she knelt by my side for the almost hour long trip. On my way to Kodiak I reclined on the comfortable padded cushions of the Albatross with Mary sitting across from me relaxing in a similar degree of well-deserved comfort. The journey had been difficult for her, too. Without the sharp pain of the contractions and the aches from my hipbones and backbones as they pressed against the hard floor surface, I was more comfortable physically, though medication was readily available had I needed it - not an option on that first flight.

The doctor checked me from time to time, but we spoke very little. Although physically pain-free, I was tired, depressed and emotionally consumed with thoughts of what had gone wrong. Why had I lost two pregnancies? Mostly I was struggling to accept the situation. I wouldn't be the only one affected by it; my family would be hurting, too.

Upon our arrival in Kodiak, an ambulance took Mary and me to the general hospital. After I was admitted, Mary told me she had friends and relatives she could stay with and would remain in Kodiak till I was released.

She wanted to accompany me on the return trip to Dutch Harbor on Reeve Aleutian.

I was placed in a double room and slept for a while without really being aware of my surroundings. Upon awakening later that day, I noticed my roommate for the first time, an Alaska Native girl. She looked quite young as she sat up in bed and smiled toward me. I said hi and introduced myself. She did the same and then asked, "Are you okay? You've been sleeping for several hours, ever since you were brought in.

I told her, "I was flown from Dutch Harbor by way of Cold Bay and it was just exhaustion or maybe they gave me something, I can't remember."

About that time a nurse showed up carrying a tiny baby. "Feeding time," she said cheerfully as my roommate reached for the infant. Then the nurse turned to me and asked, "Now that you're awake, Mrs. Brown, can I bring you something to eat? I understand you haven't eaten yet today."

"Thank you. I'm just getting oriented to where I am. I just woke up, but I guess I am feeling a little hungry." I was fully awake now, focused on going home to be with my children, Becky and Malcolm. The nurse said she would bring me a tray.

"What is your baby?" I asked my roommate.

"A little boy. What's yours?"

Of course she would not have known. "A boy, but he was a stillbirth, died during the labor." I was able to say it matter-of-factly; I was drained of tears by then. I was tired of this game, to be offered a special prize only to have it snatched from me. The first time now seemed just a tease, a prelude to this second and greater loss when I was right on the brink of receiving it. I guess I was feeling a little bitter, but I didn't want to dwell on it when the new mother appeared so cheerful.

"I'm sorry about your baby," she said in a soft voice.

"I do have two other children, though. Do you have any others?" I asked.

"Oh no, I'm only fifteen," she said, smiling. "I'm not married." She paused, as she looked down at the infant in her arms, and continued, "But I'm so happy to have my baby." And I felt happy for her. Although she was facing an uncertain, probably difficult future, she had an innocent joyful spirit which was just what I needed.

The next day she was released and as she prepared to leave, I gave her the baby items I had placed in my pre-packed suitcase – tiny tee shirts, receiving blanket, gown, and a few other baby items. I was glad that they went to someone who could really use them. She hadn't had any visitors during the time we were together.

A young looking Catholic priest stopped by my room that next afternoon. One of the nurses may have called him and told him of my situation. Kodiak (the town) was still much like the other towns in Alaska back in 1963, small and rather open; most people knew or knew of each other. He asked if he could visit with me for a few minutes. I welcomed him and asked him if he would like to sit down. It was nice to have a visitor since my roommate had left and I didn't know anyone there. I could use the distraction. We talked for a bit and I think, to relax me, he told me a bit about himself. It had only been a short while since he was ordained a priest. If I was released before the following Sunday he invited me to attend Mass and told me the time. He said the church wasn't far to walk to.

We talked about losing my baby and it helped to relieve some of my bitterness. I hadn't really talked about it. I avoided the subject and others seemed to, also, but he sounded very idealistic; the word joy comes to mind. He had a gentle happy way of expressing himself. It was hard to feel negative in his presence. He asked if I would like the baby's body moved to the Kodiak Catholic cemetery, but I declined. I was comfortable with what the Cold Bay Fire Chief said he would do. The priest said a few prayers with me, then he asked if he could visit the next day. I was surprised to realize he had been there over an hour. Whatever had passed between us, I felt much better and resolved to get on with my life and concentrate on the living.

He stayed about an hour the next day also, and I told him I would be checking out that day, to stay at a hotel while waiting for a flight that would be going to Cold Bay so I could take the DC-3 to Dutch Harbor. He said he hoped to see me at church Sunday. I wanted to see him again so I knew I would try. He also gave me his mailing address and said to feel free to write. He probably thought I needed a little more help dealing with my situation, but I already felt much better emotionally.

When I checked out that afternoon I noticed the three or four clear plastic baby bassinettes in the nursery and all had plaques attached as to who the donors were. I told the administrator I wanted to donate the expected amount to order a bassinette and have a plaque that would say 'In memory of Glen Allen Brown'. She said she would take care of it.

I walked to the nearby hotel carrying my almost empty suitcase. I had a phone number where Mary was staying so I called her and she came over and visited awhile. After what we'd gone through together on the Reeve Aleutian plane and at Cold Bay, I was in her debt for her selfless example of caring for someone she barely knew. I did not know at the time that later events would seal an even deeper and lasting friendship.

I was still in Kodiak that Sunday waiting for my flight to Cold Bay so I decided to go to the Catholic Church service. I wanted to see the young priest again as he had taken time to visit me when I really needed some spiritual counseling.

As I walked the few downtown blocks that early Sunday morning, I went past some bars. The doors were open and jukebox music poured out, accompanied by loud voices and laughter. When I glanced in I saw people sitting at the bars and the tables; it wasn't quite eight AM. It made me think of descriptions of the Wild West. Well, Alaska was known as the Last Frontier!

I made it to the church just in time and observed the kindly young priest as he went through the motions of the ancient ceremony. He had already helped me with his counseling; sitting there among those people, I knew I would be okay. I had two precious gifts back home. And I felt that now I would be able to help Charlie deal with our loss

Mary and I boarded the plane out of Kodiak a few days later. Once in Cold Bay I anxiously awaited the DC-3. Yes, I literally was looking forward to getting on it. I guess I was no longer a Cheechako, at least where flying the Chain was concerned. I had no ill feelings toward the pilots when they were unable to land on Dutch Harbor due to 'wind' on my return trip. They were careful and cautious. It had been a rough flight and I trusted their judgement.

After we bypassed the Dutch Harbor stop we flew on to Nikolski, the final stop, and spent the night there. They were set up for it and fed us boarding house style, and had sleeping accommodations, nothing fancy but always available. Aleutian weather didn't follow a flight schedule. I had been looking forward to my return home, anxious to be with my family, but the forced delay gave me time to unwind and 'get my bearings' (I think it's referred to as meditation now). I needed that private time. I hoped that the wind would die down enough to land the next day, though, and not bypass Dutch Harbor again.

Sometimes that happened. Other times, the plane could get into Dutch Harbor but couldn't land at Nikolski. When that happened, pilots, stewardesses and an occasional passenger might stay with us. Then I just moved Becky to the couch and Malcolm in with us and we enjoyed their company for dinner and breakfast. Isolated as we were, company was always welcome, though I was sorry for them about their reason for overnighting, especially passengers. On rare occasions the weather hadn't improved by morning and the unfortunate passengers were taken back to Cold Bay.

Fortunately for me, the weather was calm and sunny the next morning and the flight was smooth to Dutch Harbor. Charlie, Becky and Malcolm were at the airport waiting for me, all smiles. I had called him while I was in Kodiak and he said that he had told them about the baby and that it was in heaven. He said he returned the crib he had borrowed and removed signs of a baby showing up. I knew it was hard on him too, but I had already decided to put on a good face. I was thankful that I had Becky and Malcolm and I appreciated them more than ever.

Chapter

# 20

# Arrival of Painters

A few days after my return, two men arrived from Anchorage and moved into the bunkhouse next door, one of three that Standard Oil maintained for workers sent out there from time to time. When Charlie got home from work he told me that they would be staying about a month to paint the exterior of the five leased houses – ours, the manager's, and the three bunkhouses. Later that evening Charlie went over and invited the men to come and meet his family, since they would be our neighbors for the next month.

The two painters showed up that evening after work. They looked fairly young, maybe late twenties. The taller one appeared to be about six feet and had a heavy build. He spoke with a thick accent, though he was easy to understand. He said his name was Hans Radtke.

Curious about his accent, I asked where he was from originally. He replied, "Germany, but I haf been here a few years and I applied for my citizenship."

I was surprised at such an immediate comment after telling me where he was from. I asked, "Is your family here, too?"

"My mutter and my sister still live in Germany. I came here by myself. But I know a few guys in dis country dat are from Germany. Dey are in Anchorage, too."

The other one was shorter, though not by much, and had a slimmer build. He said he went by Rich, that his last name was Richardson. He told us he was related to The Big Bopper (J.P. Richardson), an entertainer best known for writing and recording 'Chantilly Lace', who had died in a plane crash in 1957 with Richie Valens (La Bamba) and Buddy Holly. The three had been very popular musicians in the '50s.

Becky and Malcolm, not shy around strangers, wanted some attention too, so they carried on their three-year-old and six-year-old conversations with Rich and Hans, which the men seemed to enjoy. When the men got ready to leave I invited them to have dinner with us the next evening after they finished work. They had brought some groceries with them but I knew it would not be that easy trying to fix meals in an unfamiliar place, plus Charlie and I always liked company.

The next day I watched out my front window as the painters, wearing their white work coveralls, hauled paint equipment across the street and placed long extended ladders against the side of the two and a half story 'Admiral's House'. Later I saw them high up on those ladders doing what looked like prep work. All the houses would be painted white, and they looked like they could use the paint. The frequent storms with very high winds left the buildings looking like they had been sandblasted.

That evening they showed up for dinner and stayed for a while afterward, though they both said they were pretty tired as they had worked hard trying to take advantage of the good weather. They had heard about our storms.

Rich said, "We are prepared for some rainy days and our contract only pays us when we work. We won't be working weekends, either, so we hope to spend the next two days exploring the area and maybe get someone to run us over to Unalaska tomorrow."

We didn't see them that Saturday and assumed they probably got a ride on one of the fishing boats down at the dock. When Cookie came over to play she asked Becky and Malcolm about the men. Becky told her that one was called Handsome and the other one was called Rich because he was rich!

Rich, Hans, and Fish -Front of Bunk House

Sunday morning Hans knocked on our door. When we invited him in he told us someone was going to take him and Rich over to Hog Island. A few miles east of us, it was a tiny island uninhabited by people, but there was a proliferation of rabbits with no natural predators. I don't know when or how they were introduced there. It was called Hog Island even though there were no pigs on it.

"He told us it vas practically overrun vit rabbits. Vould it be all right if I brought vun back for Becky?"

We had no pets at that time so she was very excited when she heard that she would be getting her own little rabbit. Of course, we had no objections. Hans said he would also be taking pictures while there. Charlie told Hans that there was a bad riptide in the pass but if the weather held they shouldn't have any problems. A problem did arise but it had nothing to do with the weather.

After they returned that evening, Hans knocked on our door. He was holding a tiny brown bunny. "Dis is for Becky," he said, when I opened the door. Becky was standing behind me and Hans handed her the little rabbit.

"Won't you come in?" I asked. But he declined and said he was tired and had to start work early the next morning. I would not find out till the next evening about a traumatic event that had occurred on Hog Island that day.

1962, Abandoned Military Base, Dutch Harbor

Chapter

# 21

## Hans

*The next* day, Monday, was again a clear sunny day, ideal for outside painting so the kids and I watched Rich and Hans high up on their ladders across the street with their buckets of paint, working steadily all day. However, late in the day when Charlie came home, I saw him go across the road to take a look at the progress the painters had made. They were coming down their ladders and heading for the bunk house. I watched Charlie follow them in and assumed he went in to have a drink with them before coming home for dinner. But he was only there a very short time before he left and came in the kitchen door.

The first words out of his mouth were, "Joan, you better come look at this." Then he quickly turned around and headed back out the door.

"What's going on?" I asked, surprised by his behavior.

As I followed him out the door he told me that he had noticed a thin reddish line down one side of Hans' white coveralls as he was coming down the ladder. "Then I looked down and saw what looked like blood pooling around his shoe," Charlie explained as we entered the bunkhouse and headed for Hans' room.

Hans on our Porch – Fuel Dock and Bay in Background, 1963

He was lying on his stomach in his bed with a bath towel covering his backside. There was a moist pink discoloration on it.

Charlie said, "Hi, Hans. I brought Joan over. I told you she's a nurse." Then he turned to me. "Hans had a bad fall yesterday on Hog Island. He's got a pretty large cut. I told him you were a nurse. You need to look at it."

"Hi, Hans. I would like to check it out and see what's going on." I tried to sound casual though I could tell he was embarrassed. "We have some medical supplies here so maybe we can help you."

Finally Hans spoke in his heavily accented voice as he turned his head toward us. "I tink it be okay, maybe just need a bandage."

"I'll take a look at it, then go get what we need," I replied, as I lifted the stained towel.

I took a deep breath and tried to hide my shock. Of course, I had seen far worse injuries, especially in emergency rooms, but not under these circumstances where the injured party had been working about twenty feet up a ladder all day long after incurring a huge untreated uncleaned laceration the day before with only a washcloth for a dressing. What I saw was a cut down his left buttocks about eight inches long and approximately two inches deep. It involved mostly fatty tissue and had fanned out on the sides so that it had a spread that seemed four or five inches wide. It wasn't actively bleeding but was seeping pinkish serous fluid. Even more startling than the size of the laceration was the large amount of debris on it. There were grass strands, gritty-looking gray sand mixed with a little dirt. The first thing on the list would be to remove all the debris.

"Hans, you need to go to a doctor and have this sewn up," I said, matter-of-factly, my eyes still riveted on the injury.

"No," he replied immediately and forcefully. "I just started on da houses. I need dis job. I can't leave."

I looked at Charlie and could tell he had the same concerns that I had. He said, "Maybe we can put a dressing on it and you can take the plane back to Anchorage Wednesday. Go to the emergency room and get it properly sewed up, and then come back on the next plane."

Hans surprised us both by his loud vehement response. "No! I am not leaving till I finish my job here." Then he said in an almost pleading voice, "Please just try and do vat you can, Mrs. Brown."

"Okay, Hans. We will do the best we can but if it doesn't show improvement or gets infected I still strongly advise you to see a doctor. And please call me Joan. We aren't very formal here. First I am going to clean it, wash it out good and get the grass and dirt out. How did this happen, anyway?"

"I vas carrying da little rabbit I got for Becky and I had my camera in da udder hand, so ven I started to slide on a slippery rock I couldn't catch myself because I did not vant to drop my camera. It vas pretty new and I paid a lot for it. And I didn't vant to lose Becky's rabbit; dey aren't dat easy to catch. So I fell pretty hard and rip my pants pretty bad, too."

"I think they will be easier for me to fix," I said with a smile. "I am going back to the house and get my box of medical supplies. Charlie, why don't you get a pan of warm water from their kitchen and an extra bath towel and I will be right back."

I returned a short time later and Charlie helped me clean the wound. We decided to try a butterfly-type bandage to pull the two sides together as much as possible. When I was done I gathered my supplies and also picked up the torn pants that were in a corner on the floor.

"I will get these washed and mended. I have a sewing machine so it'll be easy."

"Tanks, I did not bring very much clothes."

""I will check on the dressing tomorrow. And if you change your mind about leaving just let us know."

The next day I observed Hans back up on the two-story ladder. Well, I would be checking in the evening to see if the dressing was holding and if there was much drainage. In the meantime, I walked into a bit of a surprise in the kids' bedroom.

Chapter

# 22

# Holy Rabbit!

The bedroom door was open and as I walked past it to get to the bathroom I heard Becky speaking but I could not make out the words. When I glanced in the bedroom I saw Becky and Malcolm, both wearing their 'dress-up' clothes. Malcolm was holding the tiny rabbit while Becky poured water from my holy water bottle onto it, saying, "Mumble mumble jumble mumble."

"What are you DOING!" I exclaimed, startled at what I saw. They both looked up when I shouted at them. Becky raised the now empty holy water bottle. She innocently replied, "We were baptizing the rabbit." She seemed surprised that I had yelled at them. Malcolm just looked at me, holding the dripping creature.

"That was my bottle of holy water!" I said angrily. "You dumped it all out. Wait till I tell your dad." At the time I couldn't see the humor in removing original sin from that little animal's soul.

When Charlie came home for lunch, I was still upset over having my entire bottle of holy water dumped out. When I relayed the kids' latest antics, he replied, "Now we have a Catholic rabbit," and continued to eat his lunch. But he knew better than to laugh as he could tell I wasn't completely calmed down. Later on, though, I was able to put it all in perspective and see the humor in it and the innocence.

That evening after dinner I got the medical supplies box and Charlie and I headed next door. Rich let us in and said he was headed for the dock to do some fishing. The door to Hans' room was open and he was lying on his stomach. He raised his head and said hi to us. When Charlie asked how he was feeling he said, "Okay." Since he hadn't once complained of pain the night before I was pretty sure that was all the answer we would ever get.

After removing the dressing we saw quite a bit of watery drainage on it, but no sign of infection. So we cleaned it again and decided to leave it exposed for a little while so it could start to air dry.

"By the way, Hans, you may be happy to know that little Hog Island bunny will go to animal heaven when it dies," I said.

He looked at me, puzzled. "Do animals go to heaven?" he asked.

"Well, this one will," I said, with a smile. Then I told him what had transpired that day, and he started laughing. "Now I have to get back over there and see what they're into. Charlie will keep you company and I'll be back pretty soon to put on a new dressing."

The next night I came by myself. Charlie had had a very busy day on the dock; he started before his regular working time and ran overtime an hour. He said he'd stay home and watch the kids, which meant he'd fall asleep in his recliner chair a few minutes after I was out the door. With minimal help he always worked very long hours in the summer.

Hans was again lying down on his stomach when I showed up. He said the work had been pretty tiring, painting all day but they were having good weather and knew from everything they had been told that it wouldn't last, so they were working at a rather fast pace.

"But I don't feel bad. I tink my cut is healing okay," he said confidently.

"I'll just take a look. It's a bit soon to have a whole lot of improvement, and since you are moving around quite a bit during the day, that may pull on the butterfly bandage. You need to give this time to heal as best it can without stitches."

I proceeded to remove the outer dressing and was not surprised to see it was moist with serous drainage, though I didn't see the redness that is associated with infection. I didn't know Hans very well at the time, but was later to learn that he was the most stoic person I would ever run across. No matter how sick he might be, his stock answer was, "I'm fine," and he would proceed to act like he was, though a 'normal' person might be lying in bed moaning, taking pain pills and getting lots of sympathy, a reaction easier for me to relate to.

"I'm going to leave this outer dressing off for a little while and give the laceration (I wasn't going to call it a cut) a chance to continue to air dry. Then I'll put on a fresh dressing. I'm afraid this is a bad injury and this is just going to take a while to heal. I know you don't look forward to the rainy days but they'll give your body a rest and may help speed up the process."

"I know. It just happen at a bad time. I am glad you and Charlie are here to help me."

`I sat down on the other bed; there were two singles to a room in the bunkhouse. "Charlie won't be over. He had a typical summer day, long hours on the dock. If he's not offloading tankers from California he's fueling barges. Some are headed up North above the Arctic Circle before the ice sets in: others are bound for Shemya near the far end of the Aleutian Islands, just before Attu. So tell me, why did you leave your family and move to the U.S.?" I felt I could ask a personal question by now.

He replied with a vehemence that took me aback. "I hate Germany! I vas born in 1935 and spent my childhood in a var zone, and after da var ve had noting and just had to survive. Ven I vas older I saved as much of my money as I could and left for good on a passenger boat to Canada, den vent from dere to California mit some single German guys I met dat had da same idea. Den my new friends and I heard dere vas vork in Alaska so ve drove over da Alaska Highway to Anchorage and I got a job as a painter. I am a professional painter," he said proudly, "not like dese 'housevife painters', not like Rich. He is slow and does not seem to know a lot. I tink he got in da union because of friends."

"Well, it doesn't sound like you and Rich are very good friends."

"Dis isn't da first job ve been sent out on togeder, but I don't like vorking vit him. I end up doing more den he does because he doesn't know vat he's doing and he's slow. I vent to painters' apprentice school for four years in

Bremen. Ve vent to live dere after da var. I vanted to go to high school like my sister, but my mutter vanted me to learn a trade so I could support her and my sister who is two years younger den me. I vas just fourteen den so I had no say about it. I had never vanted to be a painter, but she sent me anyvay. I vas mad and had lots of arguments vit my mutter. She cared more about my sister, and how much money I could make for dem. It vas not hard for me to leave dem. I vanted my own life." His deep voice had become noticeably louder by the time he was finished.

Well! This was more of a revelation than I'd expected. If anger were a liquid, I could have seen it pouring out of him. How long had all that been bottled up? He must have felt comfortable telling me such personal feelings, but then the private nature of his injury may have helped to bring down those subconscious barriers that all of us carry around. A silent element of trust had obviously grown, at least in his own mind. Rather than satisfying my curiosity, though, his comments presented more questions.

"Where was your father?" He had only mentioned his mother.

"My fadder vas a baker in Konigsberg. Ven da Nazi party took over Germany and started invading countries, dey conscripted many young men. My fadder vas von of dem, and got sent to da Russian front. I vas six years old and my sister vas four vhen he vas killed in 1941. My mutter didn't have much schooling and never remarried so ve had a hard time. Dere vasn't much to eat and even going to school vas a problem. Ve spent lots of time in bomb shelters. I didn't understand a lot of tings at dat age, but I vas old enough to be scared. I am happy to be in dis country."

I felt sympathy for him, hearing his revelations of such a sad life. After having become fatherless at such an early age, dealing with a mother whom he felt was overtly partial to his sister, must have been painful, but I kept my opinions to myself and listened quietly. After a while I bandaged the wound and said I'd check it tomorrow night. Though I had made little comment he didn't act embarrassed about all his personal revelations. Perhaps, as a sort of medical professional, I represented a psychiatrist's role, allowing Hans to vent his deeper feelings uninterrupted and unjudged,.

As the week progressed, I went to the bunkhouse every evening, and visited with Hans while cleaning and airing out his wound. Remarkably, it showed signs of rapid healing in spite of his long working hours and strenuous up-and-down ladders work. I saw very little of Charlie as he spent most of his time at the dock fueling and pumping off fuel. This was our third summer here so I was prepared for long stretches of not seeing him, not expecting him for meals, not helping with Hans, nor much of anything. During those times Charlie normally ate on the boats and was sometimes gone as long as thirty-six hours, taking catnaps while one of the others spelled him.

By the weekend, I felt Hans' cut showed good signs of closing, albeit quite an interesting scar forming, so I saw no need to continue the air-dry routine.

"I will not be stopping by every evening anymore as the dressing doesn't need to be changed that much. It's looking good and I see no signs of infection. I will just make an occasional bandage check."

He looked a little hurt. "But I vill miss da visits," he replied.

I would miss the visits, too. I had found his stories interesting, though mostly sad, but sometimes funny. "You are welcome to come visit us anytime. You can check on that little Catholic bunny and see all the attention it's getting. When you see that the dock is clear there is a chance Charlie may be home and he would love to visit with you more. He enjoys company.

"Rich and I are off tomorrow so ve going to take fishing poles and try to catch a fish off da dock. If I get a fish I give it to you."

"Once in a while Charlie does that when he has time, but he's never caught anything but Irish lords, a really ugly small fish, so he just throws them back. Please don't bring me any of them."

Hans on Boat Deck at Dutch Harbor, Aug., '63

Chapter

# 23

# Ranch Talk

In 1963 there was a lingering element of distrust and/or dislike by some Americans toward Germans. Those prejudices were often deeper among family members whose relatives had participated in the Second World War. It had only ended in 1945 and some wounds were still healing. Though Charlie had family directly involved, he tended to judge people as individuals, on their own merits, rather than on their race or nationality.

When Hans showed up on the evenings Charlie was home, a friendship quickly formed, not uncommon with Charlie as he liked most people. Hans was also outgoing and friendly. They held similar views about many things, such as, people, politics and behavior. However, it wasn't long before their friendship developed into a much stronger bond. The two of them acted almost like brothers, as they spent long evenings talking about many things.

At some point in his early visits, Hans revealed that he had been looking into leasing some land that was available for eventual homesteading from the Bureau of Land Management. That information surprised Charlie.

"Joan and I have been talking about the same thing. We really like living out here. I have already been in contact with the Anchorage office, too. I'm only looking into what is available in the Aleutians. What area are you looking at?"

"I have not decided. I just vent to dher office to see vhat is available. I saw some land out here and I tink I vould like being by da vater, not be inland."

"What would you raise on the land? We want to raise sheep. They seem to do well on other ranches out here. There is an established ranch out by Nikolski and I see the shipments of wool going through here headed Outside. I'm not familiar with sheep but my dad had a Hereford cattle ranch in New Mexico. I was born on it and helped with the cattle but he sold it when I was pretty young. So I have got some experience being around farm animals, just not sheep, but I'm sure I could learn."

"Ven ve escaped from Konigsberg to Bremen, ve lived on a pig farm so I know a little about pigs, but not sheep or cows. But I tink I can learn how to raise most any kind."

As these conversations continued, the seeds of a partnership began to emerge, with serious discussions about the huge cost of such an extravagant undertaking. They revealed to each other how much each had already saved and could continue to accumulate. It sounded to me like they were committed to the enterprise and each other. Hans was easy to trust, with his habit of speaking his mind in his own blunt way. Charlie and I felt comfortable sharing our plans which suddenly moved into high gear.

We did not see much of Rich as he spent many of his evenings taking advantage of the fishing off the dock, so Hans would come over and have dinner with us. Becky and Malcolm were happy to have him around and he enjoyed their company, talking with them and playing with them, unlike some adults who tended to ignore the intrusion of children.

Since Hans spoke with a pretty heavy accent, he asked us to help him correct his pronunciation as he wanted to speak English correctly. He wanted to be as 'Americanized' as possible. He told us that he didn't like people associating him with Germany. The war had ended over eighteen years before, but the scars left by his childhood memories had never healed. It was obvious that they were pretty bad. When I would tell him how to say words correctly, he would repeat them correctly, but the next day he didn't seem to remember the corrections. He just continued to speak

'German-English'. I eventually conceded, made no more comments. Thirty years later he was still saying 've' for 'we', etc. But he never had any trouble making himself understood.

Sometime during that month of August, Fred and Jeanette left for Fairbanks with their children. Fred planned to attend the University and get his master's degree, then hoped to get back to Unalaska someday. Like us, they had similar feelings about the community. I knew that would take them a few years and we would really miss visiting with them as we had become good friends. Malcolm especially would miss their son Lowell, as the two had spent a lot of time playing together, since both had only sisters, no brothers. Fortunately for Lowell he was older than his sisters so he wouldn't have to endure playing 'girls' games like Malcolm, who was younger than Becky and Cookie.

Sadly, I knew that even if they eventually made it back, we would probably be gone. We might be homesteading on some island, though more likely, Charlie would have been transferred, probably to Anchorage. Fred and Jeanette promised to write when they were settled in Fairbanks and we hoped to see each other again sometime. But we knew it would not be any time soon.

That same month a Canadian icebreaker, the *Camsell*, appeared in the bay on its annual trip up North. We had made friends with them the previous year and were happy to see their return. The captain had invited us aboard for dinner and it appeared to be a somewhat formal setting; white table cloth, servers wearing white waiter-type uniforms and the captain and officers in dress uniforms. Charlie and I were used to a lot less formality, so this was a fun break from our 'real' world; it made us feel special though I got the feeling that the captain and officers always ate like this.

The *Camsell* would be in the bay for a couple of days and had a helicopter on board so they offered to give us rides over the island. Becky and I were able to take them up on the offer, but Charlie couldn't get time off work as this was his very busy time on the dock. There wasn't room for Malcolm plus he was also quite young, so he didn't go on the ride. He started crying when he saw the helicopter take off with his mother and sister. He could see them through the large front glass; it was taking them away. He thought we were leaving him behind and not coming back. I didn't know until we returned that he had been so upset and that he had cried the whole time we were gone.

That was my first helicopter ride and I thought it was a lot of fun, very different from an airplane ride, and Becky enjoyed it, too. It wasn't a windy day or we would not have been able to go. But seeing Malcolm's tear-stained face as he stood by the runway on our return did make me feel bad.

The physician on board the icebreaker gave me a few medical supplies, such as gauze dressings, some antibiotics and a big tin of burn salve. Whether or not I would ever need any of it, I found it comforting to have. As a parting thank you gift to the captain we gave him an Aleut basket we had previously bought from Anfesia, so flawlessly made with its perfectly woven strands of grass , it was hard to imagine the skill and patience that anyone would have to create such a beautiful work of art. But I was glad that we had something special to give him for his many kindnesses to our family. We would miss the *Camsell* when we left the island.

By the end of August Hans and Rich had finished painting the five houses; we had experienced many uncommon days that month – no rain. Though he knew he had to, Hans was in no hurry to leave. He and Charlie had become more and more focused on their monumental plans to start an Aleutian ranch. Hans gave us his Anchorage address before he left on the plane and promised to go to BLM and find out what he could as soon as he had time.

I knew nothing about ranching and had only seen sheep in children's zoos. I knew about raising chickens and that was all. I was pretty much a city girl, so I was no help in their grandiose planning, but I did get swept away in the excitement of the adventure. Perhaps I was still mentally, if not physically, operating under the influence of Richard Haliburton, a great adventurer back in the 1930s. I first became acquainted with his fascinating tales when at twelve years old I read one of his books. His influence had been so great that I felt an inner drive to follow in his footsteps. Now at age thirty, raising sheep on a remote stormy island had all the reckless appeal of a Haliburton adventure.

Chapter

# 24

# Fred Barnett

The same plane that Hans and Rich left on, brought me a special and unexpected letter from the man who had approached my stretcher at Cold Bay. I have kept the original letter these many years as a wonderful reminder of the kindness of strangers.

Along with that remarkable letter, Fred Barnett had included two snapshots of the burial site with the cross marker, one in black and white and one in color. I noticed the fencing and Orthodox cross marking the Russian lady's grave. Somehow, that made the place seem less lonely and isolated.

I was happy to be able to put a name, plus an address to the kind-hearted stranger. I wrote Fred Barnett back to thank him for all he had done for our family, though I didn't even know him. He was one of the most thoughtful people I had ever come across. Over fifty years later he remains in my memory as an outstanding example of a Good Samaritan, doing unasked what needed to be done under difficult circumstances with no expectation of a reward. This is the letter:

Cold Bay, Alaska August 28, 1963

Dear Mr. & Mrs. Brown:

We know that this will be difficult for you, but at the same time, we think "knowing" will put your mind at more ease. I made the little cross of redwood and carved the full name and date. I planted wildflowers and grass seed. The spot is very, very beautiful, high on a bluff overlooking Cold Bay. One other young person rests there. Later, a priest came through and said a blessing for your son. At the time earlier, I read the 23rd Psalm. I will visit the bluff from time to time. If you have any desires, please let me know. We trust that you are feeling yourself again. All of us have many heavy problems in life to bear but I have found that many things I have not understood the "why" at the time – always proves later that God knew best.

Sincerely,
Fred E. Barnett, Fire Chief
Cold Bay, Alaska

Glen Allen's Grave Site at Cold Bay– Fire Chief Made Cross and Planted Wild Flowers

Chapter

# 25

# Last Trip Home

As he promised, Hans wrote us shortly after he arrived in Anchorage. He thanked us for the care we gave him so that he could continue working, and also for our hospitality. He had not had time to go by BLM yet. He was given his next assignment on his return to Anchorage. He would do sandblasting on a building up in Fairbanks. He had to leave immediately as the Fairbanks winter came on very early and he would soon find himself sandblasting in minus zero degree weather. He wrote that he would check with BLM when he got back to Anchorage.

He said to tell Becky and Malcolm Hi from him. He promised to send us his new address after he got to Fairbanks as he thought he would be there for a while, longer than he was in Dutch Harbor. The letter surprised me with its good grammar and spelling. I had become used to him speaking with his 'German/English' accent and grammar. He had told us he had studied the language for a long time as he wanted to live in the U.S. as soon as he saved up enough money. We were to learn that Hans was very goal-oriented; if he made up his mind to do something he did it.

We enrolled Becky in second grade, but I did not sign up for teaching again. My mother was running out of time and I needed to be available.

Taking Becky to school in Unalaska that fall would not create such a problem this time as Becky's playmate, Cookie, would also be attending, starting first grade. Her dad and Charlie would take turns running the girls across the bay and picking them up after school, depending on the work situation.

Shortly after school started, however, during that month of September, I received a call from Sam Svarny at Unalaska that I had a marine radio call. Charlie ran me over in our skiff, and I knew before I got there that it would not be good news. My dad told me, while using the radio-phone to relay our conversation, that Mama had become much worse. She was now bed-ridden and in a lot of pain. He asked if I could return to Overland Park and help with her care. He had to keep working to pay for the mounting medical bills but someone needed to be with her at all times. As difficult as it might be emotionally, I wanted to be with her at that end-time, our last time together. There was no question about my going; I had anticipated this sad eventuality. I made immediate arrangements to book my flights and also informed the school that I would be taking Becky out for a while.

Our flight, though long was uneventful. After we reached Overland Park, I re-enrolled Becky in second grade. She was not happy about it as she missed her dad and her friends at Unalaska. At least she had a different teacher this time, plus she had plenty of cousins right next door to play with. Malcolm had just turned four that month and also spent lots of time playing with them so he didn't seem to mind the temporary uprooting.

Mama was indeed very ill and bed-ridden. She had a wonderful 'old-fashioned' doctor who made house calls, and came fairly often. Mama had spent so much time in the hospital that she was finally able to talk him into letting her be in her own home during her last months, a compassionate move on his part so that she could have family around her.

It seemed strange at the time, and still does, that I learned more about Mama and developed a deeper relationship during those two and a half months, than in our previous thirty year relationship. She spoke with me more as a close friend, one she could tell anything to. Prior to that last time home she had always maintained a dominant and somewhat critical role, maybe just thinking that was what mothers were supposed to do. I, of course, behaved like a belligerent teenager, which made it a little difficult for her to treat me any differently. As a result, we seemed to argue a lot. She had to get sick – terminally ill – before I would finally behave like a 'grown-up', and she would treat me like an adult.

Emma Calhoun
My Beautiful Spanish Mother

She told me many sad stories of a difficult childhood growing up in New Mexico. Her Hispanic parents never had much money. Their small adobe house had dirt floors and she went barefoot till she attended school. She described my grandfather as an abusive man whom she hated (her words), who beat her and her tiny mother when he was drunk. Mama had kept many unpleasant secrets from her four children. She had worked as a waitress with a minimal income but made sure my sisters and I went to private schools from the time we were five to guarantee us the best possible education, though she herself never finished grade school. She wanted us to have what she had been deprived of. At age fifty, Mama had returned to school as their circumstances improved and she fulfilled a lifelong dream to become a Licensed Practical Nurse.

As her pain intensified, I was thankful to be by her side, to help her through that final time. She died on December 2, 1963, and was buried at Santa Fe, New Mexico. We went by train to Santa Fe and had the funeral there with her relatives attending. Then the children and I headed back to Alaska. It would be good for the children and me to get back to our life as a family.

Nineteen sixty-three had been a year of sadness in my life, with the loss of my baby and my mother. That year was also the beginning of what would become two lifelong friendships with Hans Radtke and Mary Robinson. Soon I would find out nineteen-sixty four would provide its own special events.

## Chapter 26

# Back on Dutch Harbor

Charlie was glad to get his family back in time for Christmas. It had been lonely for him all those months we were gone. He knew we had to make those trips, but thankful that now it was over. Becky was happy to return to the Unalaska Grade School and since the dock was not quite as busy in the winter, Charlie had more time to take her and Cookie across the bay to school every morning. I was able to spend more time with Malcolm so I sent for a pre- school Montessori course. I wanted him to be well-prepared for kindergarten wherever we ended up.

During my absence that fall, crab fishing boats started to arrive in the bay, showing up at the fuel dock. What used to be referred to as Kodiak king crab had rapidly become known as Dutch Harbor King crab sometime in the mid-sixties, as the crab had migrated to the Dutch Harbor area waters. They had started showing up in increasing numbers before I left for Overland Park. As a result we began to experience an increased number in our island's human population, which once had been made up of only two families. Large fish processors, often over three hundred feet long, arrived as a result of the crab. They tied up at an abandoned dock that was full of big holes in its rotting wooden deck. It was located maybe a mile from the Standard Oil dock on

Verne Robinson on His Boat the *FV Ester*

the other side of the airport runway. Since it was alongside the base of Mt. Ballyhoo, we referred to it as the Ballyhoo dock. There could be a work crew anywhere from less than eighty to three hundred or more, depending on the processor size. We would occasionally see workers roaming the island; our isolation had come to an end. Company was nice but in some ways we missed the solitude. Nineteen sixty–four was proving to be a year of many changes. We were no longer so hard to find on a map; a new era had begun.

We had many fishermen up to our house for visits, drinks, and/or dinner as it was a welcome change for them to get off of their boats for a little while. In return they took us out for an occasional boat ride when they set out pots or pulled their fully loaded ones up. We only went with them when the weather was fairly calm, though they were used to rough weather. The fishermen did not hesitate to take off in weather that could only be called marginal at best; there were many boats so competition for the crab was fierce. However, the Dutch Harbor King crab smartened up and moved on to the Bering Sea, where the waters were REALLY rough – and dangerous, though that didn't give those crab much protection. The men caught on after pulling up partially-filled pots and followed them, though it made the fishing more dangerous. Those men had to be very brave and skilled to meet that challenge. I guess that was when the crab became known as Bering Sea King crab. That was probably as rough as the waters could get, so the crab had run out of preservation options.

The Standard Oil plant manager's older daughter Sharon, had returned from college in the summer of 1963. While staying at her parents' house across the street, she began dating Billy, Verne Robinson's son, by a previous marriage. He fished with Verne on the *FV Ester*, Verne's boat. At some point during the winter of 1964 they became engaged and planned to marry in the spring.

Besides the pending wedding, another event was also in the making for Verne's family. His wife Mary, my Cold Bay midwife, was expecting another baby in late February. It would be Mary and Verne's fifth child: though she had nine others and he had two. We had visited the Robinsons occasionally and Malcolm and Becky loved playing with their many children. Mary always invited us to stay for dinner and would send one of her children to their store to get anything she needed. That winter of 1964 I could not know that in the not too distant future I would make a trip to Mary's house and be confronted with a life-and-death situation.

Chapter

# 27

# Emergency

On the morning of February 27, 1964, Charlie received a call from Sam Svarny. Anfesia wanted me to go over there immediately to help with Mary Robinson's delivery; there was a serious problem, though she did not identify it. Sam said, "Verne will be over in the Ester to get Joan and run her to his house." Charlie replied, "We'll be there." Then he relayed the message to me and we went right out the door and headed for the boat dock. I didn't take the time to grab anything but my jacket, and didn't know the nature of the emergency. All I knew was that it must have something to do with the delivery.

As I stood shivering on the dock waiting for the boat I was reminded of our isolation. Without a properly equipped delivery room, many women were forced to take their chances with home deliveries or go to Anchorage eight hundred miles away and wait out their last few weeks or so. Neither was an ideal choice but partly because of the inconvenience, home deliveries were fairly common at Unalaska. Several of the local women assisted with those deliveries. Anfesia, as well as Mary, had come over to assist me at Dutch Harbor when I was in labor the previous July.

At the Robinsons' house, Mary lay quietly in a bedroom as Anfesia and some other women stood around her bed. A tiny baby was in a crib nearby, wrapped in a blanket. Anfesia approached me and told me the delivery of the infant went without any problems. Then the women waited for the placenta (afterbirth) to spontaneously eject itself, which it usually does, but as they waited it seemed like too much time had passed. Someone assisting at the delivery gave it a little tug to encourage it to slide out. Instead, the umbilical cord broke off. Anfesia said she tried to extract the placenta manually but without success. Mary started bleeding, though slowly, which indicated that the placenta might be only partially detached from the uterus, a life-threatening event if it was not removed. I told Anfesia we needed to get Mary to a hospital as soon as possible, and then relayed the information to Verne.

Verne said he would take her and me on the *Ester* to the Dutch Harbor dock. Within minutes Mary was wrapped in blankets, and then carried to his boat. He called Dutch Harbor from the boat and said Mary needed to be evacuated immediately to a hospital. He was told that, fortunately under the circumstances, the Grumman Goose, (a seaplane), was sitting on the Dutch harbor runway and would be leaving for Cold Bay as soon as the low-hanging fog lifted enough to provide more visibility. The plane would wait till we arrived, and as in my own previous situation, the pilot insisted that someone must accompany her. He would be flying alone, no stewardess, no other passengers, so Mary definitely needed someone on board to help. I told Verne I would be glad to go with her. The Goose was not our regular plane. It delivered mail and passengers back and forth to the small islands nearby that had no landing strip, and came from Cold Bay. It was headed back there that morning so we would connect with the DC-6 which had been notified of the emergency and would wait on the field and take us to Anchorage.

Verne's boat took us across the bay to the Standard Oil dock located almost next to the airstrip. Then Mary was taken to the plane and placed on its floor. I only knew the pilot, Tom Belleau, casually from seeing him at the airport occasionally when I would be at the Dutch Harbor field and he would be there getting the Goose fueled.

Mary's and my positions were the reverse of our trip to Cold Bay last summer, with her on the floor and me kneeling alongside holding her hand

– payback time. This time, the patient was quiet as she lay there not appearing to be in pain. Mary just looked at me, though I felt she must have been very frightened considering the seriousness of the situation. Tom stood in the open doorway of the plane and turned to me. I stood up.

"That fog is still hanging in there, with about a quarter mile visibility. If we wait a bit it will probably lift. How is she doing? Can we wait a while?" Tom asked.

I was so alarmed at the possibility of a delayed evacuation that I just blurted, though for his ears only, "She'll bleed to death if we don't get her to a hospital soon!"

Hearing the urgency in my voice, Tom did not say another word, just pulled the steps up, shut the door, got in his seat, and revved up the engines. I settled alongside Mary, and as I smiled at her and took her hand I said, to reassure both of us, "We'll be there soon, Mary."

She didn't answer, but maintained a calm expression, as if resigned to a situation over which she had no control. Once we were in the air the plane thankfully broke right through the fog and we had good visibility all the way to Cold Bay on one of the fastest and smoothest flights I could remember.

The DC-6 was waiting on the field for us. I ran inside the waiting room to use the restroom while Mary was being carried aboard. Tom Belleau was standing near the door of the terminal, smoking a cigarette.

He looked at me and said, "I quit smoking six months ago." He let that sink in, then continued, "I like a little more visibility when taking off; I lucked out this time, though." Did he mean he/we were flying on 'luck'? Perhaps, though I think we were actually flying on his self-confidence and skill. Many times I have heard that pilots had to make quick decisions in dangerous situations when there is no time to hesitate. I always felt that pilots had to have nerves of steel. Tom continued, "But I flew right out of the fog very quickly." I might have heard him mutter 'thank God' under his breath. He continued, "There'll be an ambulance at the airport to take her to Providence Hospital and a surgeon will be waiting there for her. I called my wife, Madeline, and she's going to meet you at the plane. I could see that you didn't have any baggage or even a purse, so she will get you settled and you can stay with us."

I wondered when he had time to note my lack of normal traveling items. I guess it went along with his general perceptiveness of a situation. I barely had time to thank Tom before rushing across the tarmac and quickly boarding the plane. With no purse, no money, and no change of clothes, I was reenacting Mary's role when she had accompanied me, though that parallel had not yet occurred to me. I barely knew Tom Belleau but his behavior was representative of many Alaskans at that time, ready to help a stranger unasked, at the risk of his own life. People often anticipated others needs before being asked, and did not consider monetary compensation.

Mary and I were in the same positions on the DC-6 as on the Goose, though there were passengers on this flight. Mary was placed on the floor and I knelt beside her. The stewardess brought me some orange juice for her. Then I put my hand behind her head and raised it enough so that she could get down some of the juice. She hadn't eaten all day, and was getting weaker from the blood loss so fluids were important. I was thankful that I had eaten breakfast before I got that morning call.

I noticed that Mary's skin had become a sallow shade of yellow while she lay on that plane floor. Her deteriorating condition was scaring me, but I tried not to show it, not wanting to alarm her.

We covered the seven hundred miles to Anchorage in record time. Because it was winter in Alaska, it was dark when we landed, though not really that late in the day. An ambulance was waiting on the field and Mary was immediately carried out to it. I descended the stairs to the tarmac and headed for the waiting room, which was near where we had landed. Madeline Belleau, whom I had never met, approached me and introduced herself, then told me she would take me straight to the hospital. I didn't even have to ask. She was as thoughtful as her husband when it came to anticipating my needs. I definitely wanted to be at the hospital.

While we both waited anxiously outside the surgery, I prayed that Mary had made it in time. Before long, a woman gynecologist came through the double doors leading to the surgery and told us Mary appeared stable though she had lost a great deal of blood and could have bled to death if she had arrived much later. The doctor said she got the placenta out but that since the uterus had clamped down on it that it could not have been removed manually. I had seen this happen before, though rarely, and knew how dangerous it was. She told me Mary was receiving the first of multiple transfusions and was resting quietly. She suggested we wait till the next day to visit her. I agreed. It had been a long day for me too, and I still had to get settled into an unfamiliar place to stay and without even a toothbrush.

It turned out that Madeline was well-prepared for me. She just happened to have a brand new toothbrush still in its wrapper, loaned me a nightgown, and said she would take me to my bank the next day to get some money. She banked at the same one so she could vouch for me. Hopefully, that would be good enough. Anchorage was still fairly small as cities go. Afterward, we would go to the hospital and check on how Mary was doing, if she was still in any danger.

I did not sleep well that night. Even though I was exhausted, I just could not get the activities of the day out of my head. I worried about Mary, how she had done so much for me when I was in a bad situation. I could only hope she got to that hospital in time. I thought of the wonderful assurances that Charlie's boss had given us, how the company would pay our way to Anchorage for medical help. Somehow, it did not register on either of us at the time that providing transportation – assuming it was available - to an emergency room four or five hours away, was not always a good enough answer. But it worked for the company, and of course I have never regretted the move to Dutch Harbor, one I might not have made had I known what they meant by 'medical help'.

The next morning we went by the bank and Madelaine identified me to the banker, who fortunately knew her by name. She explained my situation, why I had no I.D., etc. They gave me some cash and printed out some checks. Now I didn't feel quite so stranded. Madelaine was proving to be a really good new friend in a city where I didn't know anyone.

Then we headed for the hospital. I could take care of other things on my list later. When we entered Mary's room, I could see a vast improvement in her appearance. She looked so much better than she had the day before. An intravenous tube dripped blood into a vein on her arm. She said she thought she'd been getting them continuously, since the nurses just put up a new bag as soon as one was empty. I didn't mention to her that the doctor had told us she was in pretty bad shape last night, but I know she was aware of her close call. She said she was very tired as she hadn't slept much, what with the frequent blood pressure and I.V. checks during the night. We told her we would take off so she could get some rest and would come by the next day.

Madeline took me on a shopping tour so that I could buy a change of clothes and a few personal things like a hairbrush. I certainly would not have checked luggage when I returned to Dutch Harbor, just a paper sack for a purse, containing a few pieces of clothing and a hairbrush. I began to realize how it had been for Mary when she boarded that DC-3 with me last July, with nothing but the clothes on her back. There was no Madeline to meet her and take her in and it was fortunate that she had friends in Kodiak to help her during her stay.

During the few days I was with Tom and Madeline, I was treated with old-fashioned Alaskan hospitality. They made me feel right at home, though I was an unplanned visitor. Besides taking the time to chauffer me around, Madeline also had two school-age sons to look after. That short stay with people I barely knew resulted in a life-long friendship. Whenever Tom was in Dutch Harbor for more than just refueling the Goose, he came up to the house and visited with Charlie and me, and whenever I was in Anchorage over the years, I would pay them a visit. While their house was in a subdivision with houses fairly close on either side, they had a long back yard. On one of my visits, Tom surprised me with his off-time project; there was a partially constructed small airplane that he was building in that yard. It was just a city lot in a subdivision.

Once Mary had all that 'new' blood, she was ready to be released. It had only been a few days but we both wanted to get back home. We took the next available flight to Cold Bay, with plans to continue on to Dutch Harbor. Not surprisingly it was too windy for the small DC-3 to fly that afternoon, so we would have to overnight in their bunkhouse. This would not be the first time I had to do that in the three years I had lived at Dutch Harbor. However, this time the wind escalated to what we were told later was about one hundred miles an hour. I believed them because I'd been caught outside before in such winds. I knew how that felt and always got inside the nearest shelter as fast as I could.

Mary and I had to leave the bunkhouse late that afternoon to go to another building to get something to eat, since Reeve wouldn't be flying any more that day because of the storm. We hoped it would pass by the next day as we were both anxious to get home to our children. We made it to the nearby building where a dinner was prepared and saw other stranded passengers already seated at a boarding–style table. During the time we ate and visited, the storm continued to escalate. We could hear it blowing outside and weren't looking forward to our return walk to the bunkhouse. That must have been when it reached that one hundred mile per hour mark.

After barely opening the dining hall door so it wouldn't blow backward, we squeezed through and lowered our heads. We were fortunately only a short distance from the bunkhouse but we were soon bent almost double by the wind. Then when we were about eight or ten feet from the porch entry both of us were flattened to the ground, held down by that powerful force. We had to inch along on our bellies, hugging the hard-packed dirt and snow, and then reaching out with one hand till we could get a hand wrapped around the four-by-four post sticking out of the ground as part of the porch framework support. We pulled ourselves over to it and were able to rise up enough to reach the door handle, get the door open, and quickly crawl inside. While it had been a somewhat scary experience, we laughed when we got inside, maybe to relieve the tension. How ridiculous we must have looked, belly-crawling across the road, though I don't think we were considering appearances at that point. Yet another adventure Mary and I shared, though a happy one.

We talked about our two trips together. It seemed that fate had placed each of us there when the other was in her greatest need. The two events created a bond that would last a lifetime. Though gone a few years now, I truly loved Mary and miss her so much.

Chapter

# 28

# Earthquake

When I returned home in early March I learned that Verne's oldest son, Billy, and the Beal's daughter Sharon, were planning to get married later that month, just before Easter. The manager and his family would all be attending the wedding in Anchorage. Verne would accompany his son, but Mary would remain at Unalaska recuperating and caring for Irene, her new daughter. Our family would be alone on the island; March was a quiet time of year work-wise, plus Walter and Carl were also there to help. Charlie had been left in charge before, when the manager took his annual vacation. There was mostly just maintenance to take care of, clearing the roads, checking on the generators, etc.

We enjoyed those private times when we had the island to ourselves. I liked that Charlie was not so busy so we could spend a lot more time over on Unalaska visiting our friends. We often accepted dinner invitations from some of the school teachers, and also enjoyed their company with get-togethers on our side of the bay. Without television and very limited commercial radio reception, we participated in more people-related activities like dinners and conversation, another of the perks of our isolation.

The Anchorage wedding ceremony was planned for March

twenty-seventh, the Friday just before Easter, Good Friday. Our neighbors left a few days before that since they planned to spend a little extra time in Anchorage. We had just sat down to dinner on the day of the wedding when the marine radio suddenly came to life with a voice breaking through the usual ongoing boat captain conversations and static. The radio was on all the time in the background, usually on the Standard Oil frequency and it covered a large area so I usually ignored a lot of the sound, but this time it was different. That voice was loud and urgent.

The skipper on a Standard Oil tanker at the Valdez dock identified himself. That voice cut through all the background noise with an alarming report that the bay had just gone dry and that they were immediately pulling away from the dock as quickly as they could. We were stunned at what we heard and stopped eating, and then Charlie ran over to the radio to listen more closely. The dry bay was a warning sign that there would be giant waves, known as a tsunami, traveling over a hundred miles an hour, and heading for that area. That was not much warning for the tanker to make it out of the bay, nor for the large group of longshoremen who were on the dock to make it off and to the safety of higher ground. The skipper continued that they were headed for open seas as quickly as possible to try and out run the deadly tsunami. That radio burst was our first indication that Alaska had experienced a very strong earthquake. We found out later that it was the most powerful earthquake ever recorded to hit North America.

We later learned the sad news that while the Valdez tanker made it to safe waters, the dock and many of the longshoremen were not spared, along with part of the small town, The monstrous wave had reached shore and engulfed everything in its path with tremendous force as the earth continued to move and shake beneath the town of Valdez.

We stared at the radio, stunned as we tried to take in the ongoing disaster and repercussions. Suddenly the radio became flooded with reports of many related tragic occurrences coming at us in rapid-fire succession from other locations and it sounded like everyone was talking at once. One voice broke through loud and clear in the midst of all the jumbled radio traffic. This time it was the skipper on a Standard Oil tanker which was tied up at the Seward dock. He reported a situation similar to the one at Valdez and stated they were rapidly pulling away from the dock and getting out of the bay. We later learned that the entire dock and everything on it, including the office, dropped many feet straight down. Men ran off the dock to get as far away from the bay as possible. One of the men died of a heart attack while running. Because Charlie had worked there just three years before, we knew him, which made the tragedy even more personal.

Other communities in their path experienced heavy damage and some casualties. We would learn that the town of Kodiak suffered much damage, especially the fishing boats that were there.

Because the tsunami was on the Pacific side and Dutch Harbor and the town of Unalaska were on the Bering Sea side, we did not experience those deadly waves. Of course we didn't know all that at the time, so many of the people at Unalaska had headed to the high ground as a precaution. We felt safe enough in our own home as it was at the top of a small hill.

Later I thought about how we had planned to remain in Seward, with Charlie working for Standard Oil and me working at the hospital. We had even bought a house. Sometimes we had questioned whether we had made the right decision by leaving what appeared to be a stable environment, uprooting our two children and moving to a remote island. Not being in Seward when that tragedy hit provided us with an obvious answer.

We were only able to get sporadic information as we stayed up late listening to various reports. Becky and Malcolm, though quite young at the time, were aware that something really bad was happening. Malcolm, only four and a half at the time, still remembers that we let him stay up past his bedtime, an uncommon occurrence for him. He was also looking forward to seeing a giant wave.

The next day we learned a great deal more about the tragedy as news kept pouring in. The devastation to Anchorage, Alaska's biggest city, was catastrophic. We learned that the hotel where the manager's family and the Robinsons were having their wedding reception was hard hit, with a lot of damage to the building. On their return to Dutch Harbor, the Beals told us how the building swayed for a really long time and they could see some large cracks in the walls. Though no one in the wedding party was injured it was a horrifying experience to go through and a bleak way to remember a happy occasion.

In another bit of news, Val was notified by his Anchorage boss that he would be transferred in early June to Aberdeen, Washington. The new manager, due to arrive the last part of May, was a bachelor in his late forties. There would be no other children for playmates; Becky and Malcolm were really going to miss Cookie. The children had been together for three years. It would be a sad time for them as they were very close friends. Changes were happening, and there were more in store for us.

Soon after that, Charlie was told that his transfer would take place in the late fall when his replacement was due to arrive. We had known it was coming, we just didn't know when or where. Fortunately for us, it was only to Anchorage, so Charlie could continue to pursue his ranch plans one on one with Hans. They hoped to be able to get a possible lease agreement worked out with BLM. Communications had been difficult through mail and limited phone calls. He relied on Hans to provide as much information as possible till the two could go straight to the BLM office for a face-to face meeting. Hans was back working in Anchorage so he spent some time at the BLM office going over various sites and islands that were available to choose from. They all came with pros and cons, especially when two young children would be living there.

I wondered if we had enough knowledge or experience for what we planned to do, but Charlie was driven. He said he wanted a ranch, but sometimes I wondered if he mostly wanted a break from working for others. I was a very willing partner as his enthusiasm rubbed off on me, though I knew nothing about ranching, sheep or cows. I must have gotten over my previous concerns of living in some isolated place. But I still remembered that day in Seward when Charlie told me about the transfer he had been offered to go to some deserted island that I had only vaguely remembered hearing about in war news when I was a kid.

It was only April and I felt we still had plenty of time to learn as much as possible about Charlie's 'big adventure'.

*Chapter*

# 29

# Hog Island

On the first Sunday in May, we woke up to a spring morning that was both sunny and balmy, a rare combination that energizes a person to get out and do something. We decided to go for a boat ride and extend our exploration of the surrounding areas. Because windless days are not very common in the Aleutians, we thought it would be a good time to go and see Hog Island and find out if all those stories about it being overrun with rabbits were true. At least everyone we talked to, including Hans had said that it was. If so, that should be a fun trip for Becky and Malcolm.

It had been about a year since we had sold our twelve foot skiff and purchased a more seaworthy one, a twenty-two foot open wooden dory. We had used the dory for many trips to the neighboring village of Unalaska, but that was just a short run. Hog Island would be a bit of a challenge as it was at least four times farther plus there was a short pass between our island and Unalaska Island, which we would have to go through. It was well-known for its riptides which sometimes created a rough and dangerous trip when the water got stirred up. However, it was not far from the Unalaska coast near a small settlement just outside the Unalaska village, known as Captain's Bay.

I packed a lunch for the four of us as we anticipated spending a few hours over there roaming the small island. The last thing I said was, "No, we are not bringing any rabbits back." I think that might have dampened the children's enthusiasm a bit but they were still excited as they wanted to see all the rabbits they had heard so much about.

We had a smooth enjoyable trip to the island; Becky and Malcolm had always liked boat rides and this was their longest one in an open skiff. We spent the afternoon climbing all over the low terrain and watched out for the sharp slippery rocks near the beach. Hans' accident was enough of a reminder for us to be extra cautious. True to the stories we had heard there were rabbits of every shade and size that rabbits can be. It was like a giant open-air rabbit zoo. After a while we decided to have our picnic lunch, so we ate on the beach near our skiff.

While calm is pleasant, too calm is not to be taken lightly. Charlie eyed the darkening sky as we were finishing our sandwiches. "We'd better be heading back. We've got to get through the Pass over by Captain's Bay before the winds increase the riptides. I don't like the feel of the air, it's too still. I think we may be in the eye of a storm."

I could also sense the eerie stillness, having experienced it a few times on land in the three years we had been there. If caught outside I would get into the house before the swiftly approaching dark clouds opened up and let loose torrents of wind-driven water. We were a few miles away from shelter and had to cross open unfamiliar water. I grabbed our picnic things and rushed Becky and Malcolm over to the dory, and told them that we had to leave because a storm was on its way. They didn't act too happy but were always obedient children, so they climbed quickly into the dory and settled down. After Charlie pushed the dory off the beach, he then started the outboard engine. We could see our goal in the distance as we headed across the long expanse of water in a race against the rapidly changing weather. Charlie was very good at operating boats so I had confidence in him, but not the weather.

We had only traversed a short distance when the gentle waves built up to large undulating masses coming at us. Water splashed over the bow even as it rose up steeply then slammed into the trough, pouring more water in.

The only shelter on the boat was a small wood-covered area where bailing cans and rope were stored. I squeezed Malcolm inside it to protect him from the water that came into the boat, and then pulled out one of the cans. As the ocean poured into the bottom of our boat I bailed fast and non-stop, but could hardly compete with the forces of nature. My muscles felt like they were on fire, but I didn't dare let up even for a moment. Actually, I was so frightened it wasn't until afterward when we were on dry ground that I realized how sore they were.

Becky crouched in the bottom of the boat, soaked with salt spray, and held onto the wood plank seat. She seemed to be the only one enjoying the trip, as she shouted uproariously each time we pounded a wave. I wished I could share her confidence as we entered the Pass, our only way to get across the water to the nearest shore, which was at Captain's Bay on Unalaska Island.

I became even more alarmed as we entered that dark swirling mass of riptides and whirlpools and even greater amounts of water began pouring in. The boat was tossed around, both left and right, as it barely inched forward toward the faintly visible distant shore. By then, my wet hair hung in my face and my soggy jacket was thoroughly drenched with cold water. I even felt the water sloshing in my boots - and why wouldn't it be, I was standing in it. Charlie remained silent as he skillfully maneuvered the narrow dory through those crosscurrents. Sometimes the bow rose at a steep angle as the powerful waves battered us from what seemed like all directions. Other times we just bounced up and down in what felt like one spot, not moving forward, as if we were stuck. But at least we were still afloat, and Becky was still shouting happily. Malcolm, at age four was bravely silent, more stoic like his father. My own silence was not due to bravery. I just wasn't doing my praying out loud.

At last we were back into protected water, safely headed for the beach at Captain's Bay. The waves were still fairly big, stirred up a bit by the storm, but they were not coming at us from every angle and I began to relax a tiny bit mentally and physically. I had been bailing so fast that I think I had been holding my breath a lot, because I started taking in big gulps of air now that the dory settled down and water quit pouring in. To put that trip in perspective, what should have been a twenty minute trip from Hog Island took almost two hours.

When we reached the Unalaska shore we saw a few people standing on the beach wearing rain gear. As Charlie ran the boat up to the shore in the shallow water I leaped over the side into water that was almost to my knees presumably to grab the line, but mostly I just wanted out of that boat.

Someone on the beach yelled, "What are you doing out in this storm? Are you crazy?" Then he helped tie the boat up, while we tried to explain our ignorance of what it meant to be in the eye of a storm while going through riptides in the Pass. The people invited us into their home to get warm and have some welcome hot tea. We were so wet that we weren't sure how we could accept the invitation without magically wringing ourselves out first. Fortunately we were able to leave a small pile of our sodden clothes in their arctic entry which was designed for such items, then entered the wonderfully warm room. After we had settled down and were holding the hot cups, they started laughing at us. But I was still tense. In my own mind I felt we had just come through a near-death experience. I would be able to laugh later, much later. In retrospect, I realize they weren't laughing about the real danger we had been in, but at our ignorance of the weather. If the weather seems too good to be true, don't take a long trip in an open wooden boat, much less through a dangerous Pass.

Unlike their mother, Becky and Malcolm were not traumatized by the experience. Instead, they acted as though it was a great adventure, fun and exciting. I was getting no sympathy from anyone. I guess I was just too old to have found it 'fun'. However, in time I would experience worse, more challenging, and far more dangerous Passes. Just knowing that I got through this one was a helpful memory I could fall back on – sort of like that first DC-3 plane ride into Dutch.

Chapter

# 30

## Andy

The new manager, Andy, arrived the last week in May; he looked to be in his late forties. He was built a lot like Charlie – stocky and medium height. His silver hair was cut in short bristles, pretty much the style that Charlie had adopted except that his hair was Cherokee black, thanks to his great grandmother. Another similarity, he was a friendly, cheerful guy with a good attitude. Charlie liked him immediately and looked forward to a smooth transition of managers. Andy was assigned to live in the very spacious 'Admiral's House,' once it was vacant. In the meantime, he moved into the bunkhouse next door where Hans and Rich had stayed, since the Beals were not scheduled to leave till June fourteenth.

Andy was a bachelor so there would be no family joining him. Standard Oil had apparently changed its policy about preferring to send family men. When Charlie was offered the position to that location, he was told he was picked because he had a family. Management seemed to think that would help the employees endure the perceived loneliness and isolation, and stated they would only leave us there for three years. Some visiting employee must have ratted us out about how there was nothing lonely or isolated about the place.

The three weeks would give the departing manager time to orient Andy, and Charlie could also help as he had taken over those duties whenever the manager had been gone. While it was the busiest time of the year, Charlie, Walter and Carl were seasoned workers and they always put on a few extra guys in the summer, so there were no anticipated problems with the changeover.

However, there is always a chance for unexpected problems. At about eleven P.M. on the night of June 1, shortly after we had settled down for the night, Charlie received a phone call from the outgoing manager across the street. He had just received a call from Unalaska that the Albatross, the Navy rescue plane out of Kodiak, was on its way to Dutch Harbor to pick up a woman being brought over from Unalaska. Someone had reported to Kodiak that she was in labor and was vomiting blood and should be evacuated to a hospital. The Albatross was due in less than an hour when Val got the call and notified Charlie. Why such short notice I don't know.

We had lived at Dutch Harbor since 1961 and no plane had ever landed at night, and for a very good reason - there were no lights on the runway. Charlie was instructed to alert Andy and the two of them were each to take a company truck down to the airfield and park facing each other at opposite sides of the head of the runway, with their headlights on. That was the best plan they could come up with to aid that incoming craft on short notice late at night. While it was the first of June, our daylight hours were not as long as other parts of Alaska; we were much farther south of the well-publicized 'midnight sun' area that Alaska is noted for.

Dutch Harbor at midnight seemed very dark when I heard the loud roar of the plane. From what I could see from our house on the hill, its lights appeared to be making a very low approach toward where I knew the airstrip would be. Not long after, I quit hearing the sound of the engine.

As I kept watching out the front window I saw a vehicle come up our road from the opposite direction, from the direction where the boat landing was. I figured it must be the people from Unalaska. The truck stopped in front of our house and I went out to meet it. They had the woman who was in labor with them. I told them I thought the plane had just landed and the

Dutch Harbor Runway – Early '60s, Between Two Beaches

doctor would probably be up to the house shortly. I led them to the bunkhouse next door where Andy was staying and had them take the sick woman to the other bedroom to await the doctor.

Soon I saw the headlights of the two company trucks coming up the road from the airport, then they stopped out front. I watched outside while Charlie climbed down from his truck along with some men in uniform. Then I became somewhat puzzled as I saw a soldier get out of the driver's side of the other vehicle while another one got out of the passenger side. Just as I wondered where Andy was, if perhaps he had remained at the airfield, I heard loud unmistakable moans of someone in pain. Val had come outside and approached the second truck. As I walked toward it I was startled to see several men lift Andy from the truck bed on a stretcher. From his obvious discomfort, I figured he must have had an accident. Charlie directed the men carrying the stretcher to the bunkhouse and the rest of us followed. I said nothing as I knew Charlie would fill me in later.

The military doctor and some of the servicemen placed Andy on his bed and then examined his leg. It appeared to be at an unnatural angle, dislocated and a possible fracture. After the doctor and some of the men worked quickly on it before the swelling made it more difficult to get the joint in place, he ordered the men to get Andy ready to evacuate as soon as they could take off and get him to the hospital.

He turned to Val and Charlie and told them, "We'll be taking him with us to Kodiak as this man needs immediate attention. Then he will probably be transferred to an Anchorage hospital. Is the woman that is vomiting blood here yet?"

"Yes, she is in the other room with her midwife and family members."

The doctor left to check on the situation he had originally come for while some of us stayed with Andy. Charlie gathered a few things for him as he would be leaving on the plane. Andy was still in pain but quieter.

The doctor returned to Andy's room and told us they would not be taking the woman with them. After examining her he determined that she was not actually vomiting blood but that she had experienced some blood streaks from her irritated throat after so much retching. He felt that otherwise she was in no apparent danger and told her not to be alarmed by the blood streaks. Her labor still had a ways to go but he offered to take her with them anyway. However, she decided to remain at Unalaska with the midwives. She had other children at home and wanted to be with her family.

I could sympathize with her original fears, knowing how unequipped we were in serious medical emergencies. Mary's traumatic delivery was still fresh in my mind. I didn't know what had caused Andy's accident, but I knew I would find out from Charlie as soon as everything settled down.

The doctor and his men, carrying Andy on the stretcher, went back to the trucks with Val and Charlie and returned to the airfield. Again the pilot would have to rely on truck headlights, which Val and Charlie manned.

After the plane took off, Charlie returned home. Now it was the middle of the night; I would finally learn what had happened.

"Right after Andy and I had parked on opposite sides of the head of the runway with our headlights on, I heard the plane. It sounded very loud and its lights appeared low and close, so low it looked like it was swooping right down on us, I thought it might even hit our trucks. Andy must have been of like mind. Without any communication between us, we both opened our doors and leaped out, and then I ran toward the side of the runway. I flopped on the ground just as I heard the thundering roar of the big plane hit the tarmac. It came to a stop shortly before they reached the end of the runway. Good thing or they would have ended up in the bay."

"But what happened to Andy?"

"Well, as I adjusted to the plane's noise I heard these loud screams. I knew it had to be Andy. I ran across the field and saw him lying there yelling that he'd broken his leg when he jumped out of the truck. I could see his leg was at a peculiar angle. I told him I would run over to the plane and get some help. I felt bad leaving him as he seemed to be in a lot of pain, but there was a doctor on board and that's what he needed. I ran toward the guys yelling 'Help' as they were coming down their stairs. I told them what happened and raced back over to Andy with them following. What an awful way to start his new job. I hope he can get back soon."

The next day the outgoing manager said he had told his boss what had happened, but he was told that the plans were unchanged. He would still leave for Washington on June 14, and Charlie could take over till Andy was well enough to return. More help could be hired from the village as work picked up, which was usually done anyway. It did feel different though with no family across the street in that large house. Having lived out there those past three and a half years had changed my attitude about isolation, however. We weren't exactly hermits and we both liked visiting people, but there is something to be said about solitude; it doesn't have to equate with loneliness.

We later learned that Andy was in an Anchorage hospital and would be unable to walk for at least two months. I felt really bad that he had suffered such a serious injury. He hadn't even had time to settle in. Though it might be awhile, we still looked forward to his addition to our dwindling population of four.

Chapter

# 31

# Ranchers Arrive

June was turning into an unusual month. After Andy's dramatic departure an event we had been expecting occurred that first week. We had previously learned from newspaper articles that friends sent us in May that unbeknownst to us another family had a plan parallel to our ranch plans, though on a much larger scale. A family from near Miles City, Montana, the Choates, had sold their ranch and leased part of Unalaska Island, about 250,000 acres, over a third of the island, from the Bureau of Land Management. Rufus and Alice Choate and their three children planned to establish a sheep and cattle ranch along with a few other farm animals - pigs and chickens.

When we first heard the news we were surprised that another family who did not even live in Alaska had done their own research and were making the giant step. They had purchased an old ninety-five foot wooden boat and turned it into a Noah's ark to transport hundreds of animals, sailing from Seattle on the over two thousand mile journey. That seemed like a pretty brave thing to do.

Charlie hoped to meet them and maybe get some information on what he and Hans planned on doing. Unfortunately for Charlie, it was his busy time. When the stock boat arrived just outside the village of Unalaska, he was working long hours on the dock, night and day, with a steady stream of tankers and barges arriving. In the meantime, the manager was busy packing, getting his family's belongings ready to ship. While there was no time to make contact with the new ranchers on their arrival, it was at the top of Charlie's list as soon as he could get a break. He was glad for all that extra overtime, though, as it would be his last summer on the Dutch Harbor dock. His Anchorage transfer was just to the International Airport where he would be fueling planes, an outside job in below zero temperatures, and no chance for overtime. The summer of '64 was his last opportunity to add to our nest egg.

We were unable to get over to Unalaska that June but Charlie brought home news from the guys that worked with him. They told him that only eighty sheep were on the first trip, along with some other animals and lots of supplies, and that the Choates were going back to Seattle to bring up more sheep right away. They said that in the meantime, the Choates had let the animals out to graze up the valley just outside of town where they had rented a place. They had not known that the town had several half-starved dogs that ended up killing at least eight or nine of the sheep which had roamed into town. They were all over the roads, in yards and in open storage sheds and the townspeople weren't very happy about the disruption. But the family had such a mountain of work to do upon arriving that it was going to take time to get settled in. It certainly gave Charlie and me a lot to think about in our own planning.

The first part of July we finally got a chance to go to Unalaska as I needed to do some shopping, and Charlie needed a work break. We saw sheep roaming the streets sort of looking like the proverbial lost sheep, while others were lying beside some of the buildings. This scene was what we had been told to expect. This was a particular farm animal I had never seen close up except through car windows or petting zoos. They looked pretty cute to me, just like their pictures, with their simple blank faces. They appeared gentle, not trying to bite people or chase them. I thought then that if we did get our ranch lease it might be fun raising them. Their helpless, defenseless behavior made me feel sorry for them but lots of villagers were understandably a bit unhappy about this sudden deluge of creatures in their yards.

Rufus Choate, Wife Alice, Son Ted, Friend Dale Lott on *MV Robert Eugene*

We learned the Choates were staying up the valley just out of town, so we went by to meet them and tell them of our similar plans. Charlie and Rufus immediately hit it off as both were of similar outgoing temperaments. Rufus seemed happy to share his knowledge and suggestions with Charlie and they made plans to get together more often when they both had some free time. Having so much negative input from the village, I imagined Rufus appreciated talking with someone who approved of what he was trying to accomplish, and had hopes of starting a similar undertaking. Maybe Rufus felt some validation for his gutsy venture.

Charlie was energized after that visit. Every free chance he got we found ourselves back at the Choates. Our plans were coming together at an accelerated rate for such a massive undertaking. Meeting the Choates was the biggest break we'd had so far. I should mention his wife, Alice, was very much a partner, but where Rufus was outgoing around us, she was reserved. I was reserved for a different reason. I had almost no knowledge of what all ranching entailed, what it would be like, to take care of animals other than dogs and cats, what it would be like to take a long boat trip. My longest boat ride to date had been the almost disastrous return from Hog Island, and that had been only a few miles; now we were talking about several thousand. I was the third partner and would have a say, too, but I didn't know what to say and certainly didn't know what I was getting into. I only hoped Charlie and Hans knew what they were doing as I watched it all unfold.

I wrote Hans about our visit, and while this was his busy time also, he wrote back that he was ready to go with whatever we decided to do. I promised him that I would keep him informed about what all transpired between Charlie and Rufus Choate, so that he would be kept in the loop.

I did not have any serious doubts, like I did when we considered our initial move to Dutch Harbor. My main focus now was that it was a way to stay in the Aleutians. I can't explain my feelings, just that I saw it sort of as my 'magical kingdom.'

Chapter

# 32

# Saying Goodbye

In the first part of August Andy returned to Dutch Harbor and moved into the large 'Admiral's' House' across the street. We were saddened to see that he had a limp and had to use a cane to get around. He said he would probably need it from now on. According to his doctor it had been a very bad injury. He was barely middle aged but circumstances have a way of creating life changes. Charlie was glad that Andy was back and would be taking over the managerial duties, even though he now had some physical limitations.

When Rufus Choate was back from his restocking trips and caught up on his shearing projects, or whatever his ranch situation demanded of his time, Charlie visited him every chance he could get away.

Charlie also was in more contact with Milt Holmes who ran a huge sheep ranch on Chernofski. Milt was a very friendly and helpful man who gave Charlie various bits of advice. He recommended purchasing Columbia sheep, which he said did well in the local climate. The Choates must have also known that as it was the breed that they brought.

We were getting closer to the possibility of a ranch, so Charlie worked every hour he could get in, to the point of exhaustion though extra help from the village lightened some of his load. We were spending very little money, saving every penny for the ranch. Additional overtime brought on by unfortunate circumstances, along with the financial help Hans would provide was not only welcome, but needed.

Hans's appearance on the scene just when we needed someone of like mind seemed providential in retrospect, just like the unexpected arrival of the Choates. We both felt a sense of the rightness of our leap into the great unknown. The many coincidences erased our feelings of self-doubt. More than ever we felt compelled to act on those remarkable concurrences of events.

While our lives were still in flux, one thing was certain: we would be moving to Anchorage in late fall. I planned to go on ahead of Charlie with the children, and rent a place for us, partly so that we would have somewhere for all our belongings to be sent, so I was busy with sorting and selling and packing our things. While the company would be shipping them, we wanted to keep only what we needed. We hoped to pick up a few second-hand pieces of furniture in Anchorage just to help us get by till we would leave for – somewhere. If we were eventually to move to some island we did not want to transport unnecessary items. I posted signs on the store walls in Unalaska and listed lots of items for sale, including our furniture. We hoped that what did not sell would be bought by Charlie's incoming replacement, though we did not know if that would be a single person like Andy, or another family. Like us, the villagers lived in semi-isolation so they welcomed the opportunity to have some of our things available to purchase.

While we still had not settled on any one particular island of those available, we had several good prospects based on information from Hans so we were able to narrow it down. The one that interested us the most was Akutan. Though we had never been there, the fact that it had a village and was only forty miles away from Dutch Harbor attracted us. Also, the island of Akun was very near it and was also available. We liked the fact that there were some nearby choices. We hadn't wanted to get too far away from Rufus Choate's protective mentoring. We also thought that perhaps we could visit our Unalaska friends, though we would be separated by about forty miles of some pretty rough waters, and of course we only had our dory. Anyway, it was another plus in picking Akutan.

When the school year began in September, we took Becky over to Unalaska and enrolled her in the third grade, though we knew she would be in for yet another school transfer in a few months. I was glad that she would get some time to be with her Unalaska class mates before we left; she had known them since first grade. Not knowing where we were heading in the future she could not know when she might see them again. Her constant playmate/companion for over three years, Cookie, had left the island a few months before, so she had already parted from one close friend. Becky was very resilient but I felt that spending those last remaining months attending the Unalaska school was important for her. Andy assured Charlie that there was no problem allowing him to transport her back and forth every day as long as the work got done and he gave the company at least eight hours of his time. When Charlie could not make it to pick her up on time the teachers, who were also our friends, let her stay with them till he could get over. She was a very good student and I was glad that despite the various interruptions in changing schools during the past few years there had been no problems with her grades. Making and losing friends was probably the hardest part.

Charlie and I would have the same problem, leaving our friends of the past three and a half years to start a new life in an undecided place, not knowing when we might see them again. I knew I would miss our visits to Mary Robinson's house, to Gert and Sam Svarny's, to Anfesia's, our teacher friends and many others. We would also miss the close friendly lifestyle that came with living near a small isolated community. Whether our grandiose ranch plans ever materialized or went the way of bonfires - up in smoke, we had no choice about this immediate move. Charlie was required to transfer and to the biggest city in Alaska.

In October, Charlie and I made one last trip together to the village to say good-by. I felt worse doing it than I had expected. After almost four years living in Dutch Harbor, I really did not want to leave.

Now our focus was on our major move to Anchorage. We were also very involved in attempting to finalize our ambitious plans for an Aleutian sheep ranch, especially now that we had the good fortune of the appearance of the Choates and their generous offer to help us.

Then around the middle of October, I was surprised and saddened when I received a letter from a woman I had never met, Mary Ann Barnett, the wife of Fred E. Barnett, the Cold Bay Fire Chief. He had been the person who had so thoughtfully taken baby Glen's body from the aide station and buried him. He had also hand-made and erected a white cross, then written the beautiful comforting letter to me.

In the midst of her own sorrow, she took the time to let me know that the man who had performed such unique acts of kindness toward me had died suddenly of a heart attack at the age of fifty-eight while attending a two-alarm fire at the power house just after midnight on September 9, at Cold Bay. That terrible incident had happened a little over a month before, though Charlie and I had heard nothing about it. We didn't get the Anchorage paper, which had reported it and there was no TV there in those days. I had hoped I would get to meet him and thank him in person when going through Cold Bay while waiting for the DC-6 to take us to Anchorage. I immediately sent off a letter of condolence, and thanked her for letting me know, again expressing my gratitude for her husband's thoughtfulness. I never heard from her again, though a month later when the children and I were going through Cold Bay in mid-November, I asked about her and was told she had already moved away.

Years later I was able to assist in honoring Fred Barnett's memory as a result of the letter that he had sent to me over fifty years ago, but more on that later.

Chapter

# 33

# Anchorage

When the children and I arrived in Anchorage that November, we would be waiting for Charlie to join us. It was to be only a temporary move before we could get a lease site back in the Aleutians, so I rented a small duplex close to everything. As our many boxes kept showing up, we stacked them higher and higher in the tiny living room. With all our belongings sharing that place we barely had room to get around. Thank goodness we had been able to get rid of as much as we did before leaving Dutch Harbor.

I bought an old car - really old, $300 – that burned more oil than gas. It was just so I could get around, plus Charlie would need it also as soon as he got to town and started work at his new job. I just hoped that it would last until we were ready to leave once we had a lease in place, wherever it might be. I did not know about the oil problem when I bought the junker. I had never known much about cars, so it was pure necessity that I was entrusted with that purchase.

As soon as we were settled I enrolled Becky in the third grade at Willow Crest Elementary School so that she would not miss very much. Free kindergarten was not available so I enrolled Malcolm in a private Montessori school for kindergarteners, Tom Thumb School, since he had turned five in September. I hoped to take as much advantage of the schools as there was time for. I had no idea where we would be if our plans materialized. Probably we could end up in another isolated area where there were no schools and I would be homeschooling them.

We were soon joined by Charlie and he started his new job at Anchorage International Airport fueling the big commercial planes. Maybe Standard Oil had got word of his new plans, which could explain why they assigned him to such an unpleasant position. Outside work fueling planes during the Alaskan winter with its below zero temperatures sure didn't make anyone want to make a career of it. In its own way perhaps the job helped him to resolve some of his doubts about giving up the steady paycheck. He was still young and if he was going to make the break the time was now. He and Hans had done so much groundwork that they were very close to making it become a reality. Now that all of us were in Anchorage, getting a lease was the final hurdle before we could move forward.

With the children now enrolled in school and all of us in Anchorage, I went to work as a registered nurse at the local psychiatric hospital, Alaska Psychiatric Institute, commonly referred to as API. My first job out of nurses' training had been in psychiatry, first in St. Louis, then Kansas City. After moving to New Mexico, I did a variety of types of nursing, but not psychiatry. So I was happy to get back into what had once been my first love. My shifts worked well with Charlie's so we were both able to help with the children and share the car.

Hans spent most of his free time with us at the tiny apartment so we decided to move to a larger place where we could all be under one roof, plus cheaper than renting two places. It would be easier to go over plans as we would have more time together. We would also find out how compatible we were on a day to day basis, something it would be good to know before embarking on this major venture. After all, we might end up spending the rest of our lives living and working together, pooling all of our resources - money, possessions, labor – whatever would be needed for this operation to succeed.

In January we rented a large house in the Sand Lake area of Anchorage. It came with a garage, so we moved our many boxes into it. The small duplex had left no place to sit down except in the tiny kitchen. Hans moved all of his belongings into the house, also, though naturally he didn't have as much as a family of four. Nevertheless, we could already see that all of us were going to have to get rid of more stuff.

Of course, we now lived in a different school district so Becky experienced yet another change in schools, her third that school year. Thank goodness, she was an adaptable and smart student. Her love of reading probably helped, also. With ex- teachers for parents, she also had a pro-learning home environment so she continued to make high grades and also became an exceptional speller. With her outgoing nature and flexibility, she made yet more new friends.

It was a friendly neighborhood with lots of young couples and children. It wasn't long before all of us had made friends with many of them and were invited to their get-togethers, where they pelted us with frequent questions. I think our big attraction was the unique plan of three greenhorns with children in tow, embarking on a major adventure into the unknown. Some years later some of them were still good friends with us.

Chapter

# 34

# The Lease

Charlie often worked the late shift at the airport which allowed him to spend time during the day with the Bureau of Land Management and check out the available parcels in the Aleutians. If anything was going to happen it had to be soon, but there was so much still to do. By then, he and Hans had it pretty much narrowed down to a few of the available choices. Though more isolated than Dutch Harbor, Akutan seemed to have the most to offer. There was an Aleut village (a Native Reserve) with a population of ninety in the 1960 census. It had scheduled plane service from Reeve Aleutian Airways. Though there was no runway, a sea plane landed on the water then taxied up to the beach by the community bringing and picking up mail and passengers. It was the Grumman Goose, the one Tom Belleau had flown to Cold Bay with Mary and me. However, its schedule was only every three weeks and could be even more erratic than what we had experienced at Dutch Harbor over the years because the sea plane also had to deal with rough water and frequent fog.

That was a known problem and we had already managed to adapt to dependent-on-weather plane services over the years. Akutan also had a school in the village, unlike some of our other possibilities. We also thought that perhaps we could find a place to rent if one was available, and the children could attend classes while we built our cabin somewhere on the island. So the three of us agreed; we wanted Akutan.

Charlie and Hans began the application to lease about half of Akutan Island, making sure part of it bordered the village property so that we would not be cut off from it. During the process the guys thought that they might like to lease the island of Akun, also, thinking it might serve better to put some of the animals on it, away from any village dogs. The BLM said it would not cost that much more to lease, so it sounded like a good plan. Long story short, the would-be ranchers applied to lease all of Akun and half of Akutan.

They had stayed in close touch with Rufus Choate and he agreed with the idea of two separate islands. He reminded them of the troubles he had at Unalaska when he unloaded his sheep a little too close to a community, especially one with dogs. We were working with a pretty tight budget so we really could not afford to sustain the initial losses that he dealt with if we were going to make it. Hans and Charlie completed paper work for both parcels and were told that approval was likely and should not take very long.

The acceptance came very quickly. They must have felt we had a chance to succeed, though I am not sure what they based it on. It certainly was not our ranching experience! But I was just as excited as Charlie and Hans about the prospect of doing something 'different', though mainly I just wanted to return to the Aleutians. This time it was with the hope of making it my permanent home. In the short span of a few years all my reservations about leaving the mainland with its many advantages and facilities that I had grown up beleaving were necessities had vanished. While forced to be more self-reliant and less dependent, to my great surprise I actually enjoyed it.

As soon as the approval came through in late winter, Rufus Choate joined us in Anchorage and set about helping us to come up with what appeared to be a realistic list of necessities. The list included affordable numbers and types of animals, the amount of bagged feed and hay needed, and many other supplies, such as wool bags, the type of shearing instruments, etc. This is a good place to mention that neither Hans nor Charlie had ever seen a sheep sheared. Again Rufus had already come to the rescue in that department, as his daughter's fiancé, Jack, was an experienced shearer

Charlie Meeting Me at Seward, 1965

and would train and help them. He was also familiar with operating the old freighter. He had made the previous trips as first mate on the *MV Robert Eugene* and planned to make this summer's trip also.

We could see that this operation would cost us most of our savings, so we applied for a special five year loan that only had annual payments, designed for farmers and ranchers in Alaska. It was only for five thousand dollars but in the mid-sixties that was a lot of money, at least to us.

The guys gave Rufus the go-ahead to place our order with a stock broker in Montana. We had no thoughts of cold feet, only the excitement of the adventure. They ordered four hundred Columbia sheep, fifteen Hereford heifers, one pedigreed bull, and two horses. The animals would be trucked to the dock at Seattle in May for a target date of departure in early June for the Aleutians. By now it was the early part of April.

The Choate family was getting ready to leave for Seattle to prepare the *MV Robert Eugene* for the trip to Unalaska and Akutan. They had agreed

Joan on *MV Robert Eugene* at Seward, 1965

to lease the boat to us but deducted some of the cost for their own usage as they planned to bring a little more stock and supplies for their own operation. Nevertheless, it would be a very expensive trip.

Charlie gave Standard Oil his notice the first of April so that he could take off as soon as possible for Seattle. Hans had already quit his painting job and was ready to leave. Once there, they were going to be very busy purchasing a great deal of supplies and feed. The Choates planned to be there already and would provide invaluable assistance as to what all might be needed. I was a little overwhelmed with the thought of what was clearly a very large – and pricey – load. But there was no turning back, and I did not want to. I would remain in Anchorage till the school year ended, then finish the packing and head for Seward with Becky and Malcolm. The boat was expected to arrive at the Seward dock sometime around the middle of June. Then we would board along with all of our earthly possessions.

Chapter

# 35

# A New Adventure

When the school year ended for Becky and Malcolm, I quit my job at Alaska Psychiatric Institute and contacted my old friend in Seward, Babe Blue. She was the hospital administrator at Seward General Hospital, where I had worked before moving to Dutch Harbor in 1961. She offered to let us stay with her and would take us to the dock when the boat got in. I finished the last of the packing and friends helped me load all those boxes and transported us to Seward.

Our timing was pretty close so we were not in Seward more than a couple of days before I received word that the *MV Robert Eugene* had reached the Seward dock. So Becky, Malcolm and I, with everything we owned, headed for it. This would be the biggest boat I had ever been on. It was so much bigger than those open skiffs I had experienced previously, so I felt no misgivings about making the long trip out the Chain, sometimes through rough waters. The boat had a picturesque look which defied its age, with its freshly painted white hull and green trim. I could only hope that the confidence it inspired in me was well placed. I would soon find out.

Charlie came down the gang plank all smiles to greet us that clear sunny day, June 24, 1965. It was somewhat reminiscent of our arrival on Dutch

Harbor, April of 1961, when I experienced that same happy greeting. A few things were opposite though. We were happy travelers, and not stinking of vomit nor being buffeted in the face with cold needles of sleet. This time the weather was sunny and warm, the three of us were excited to see Charlie and we looked forward to embarking on our long-awaited new adventure.

Charlie, Hans and several others carried our belongings from the dock and stowed them down in the hold where there was still a bit of room in a very crowded boat. I bid Babe Blue, a true friend, goodbye and thanked her for her hospitality and for her help.

The boat pulled away from the Seward dock that afternoon, sitting low in the water, headed for its next stop, Kodiak Island about twelve hours away. We were going to pick up a pregnant Australian Sheep Dog there from a rancher who would meet us at the dock. The Choates had been in contact with him and we were offered two of the expected litter. The Choates would keep the rest, returning the female to him on their next trip Outside. After Kodiak the next stop would be Akutan, a long journey for a boat full of animals.

I stood on the deck and breathed in the cool smell of the sea on that balmy afternoon. I would have plenty of time in the days ahead to contemplate how I ended up on a seventy- five year old retired Seattle fire boat bound for a semi-remote island in the Aleutians that I had never seen, but had planned to make my permanent home. Four years before, I had huge misgivings about such an undertaking. This time I could barely restrain my excitement; it was happening. We were going back to the Chain. As an equal but silent (sort of) partner, I was a rancher-in- training, no turning back now. Our dream had become a reality.

Dr. Michael Livingston, PhD. *Photograph Courtesy of KiliiiYuyan, Photographer*

Chapter

# 36

# A Final Note

When I began writing about our early days at Dutch Harbor, I wanted to find out if Glen's burial site at Cold Bay was considered a cemetery and had a name. With another grave already there I thought that by now there might be more, since over fifty years had passed.

In my search I came across an internet site called Find a Grave. I was happy to discover that there was in fact a cemetery at Cold Bay and its name was Trout Creek Cemetery. I also discovered that Michael Livingston, PhD, who I did not know at the time, had placed some information and pictures of Glen's burial site on a page in Find a Grave. I contacted Michael and found out he had been tending Glen's site for a very long time, about five years. I gave him further information to include on the site as most of the posting was hearsay and speculation since little was known about Glen Allen Brown, actually nothing except his date of death.

I was curious to know what his interest was in the grave and discovered a lot more about the cemetery and the fireman who had buried Glen. Michael himself wrote that he was raised on Cold Bay and his mother is buried in the cemetery, which is actually located on his family's homestead. Since it was pertinent to the story, I wrote him explaining the entire incident:

how Glen came to be buried there and the story of my delivery experience, including the part Fred Barnett had played in making the cross and burying the baby.

When I shared my information about Fred Barnett, including the letters he and his wife had sent me, Michael shared additional information. He and his brother and sister had been children back in 1964 when Chief Barnett died of a heart attack while putting out a fire in the middle of the night. Michael's family had been good friends and ended up with the Barnetts' dog, a big black lab named Pupule. When I asked what kind of name that was he informed me that it was Hawaiian for 'crazy'. Pupule liked to eat cigars and drink whiskey!

Michael had not known about Fred Barnett's special kindness to me, a stranger. He felt, along with me, that Fred deserved some recognition for the kind of person he was, both because of his actions toward me and due to the fact that he died a year later in the line of duty. Michael is an expert researcher and was able to locate the 1964 newspaper article regarding the fire and the fireman's death. He proceeded to get paper work to apply for Fred's entry into the National Firefighters Memorial. The research and patience required a great deal of digging (months) to gather the necessary information.

As a result, thanks to Dr. Michael Livingston's perseverance, on September 11, 2016, fifty-two years later Fred Barnett was honored in a ceremony in Anchorage, at the Alaskan Fallen Fighters Memorial, attended by firefighters from around the state. He was also nominated for the National Fire Fighters Memorial - all of this as the end result of a generous act of kindness for a stranger.

FREDRICK E. BARNETT
FIRE CHIEF
COLD BAY FIRE DEPARTMENT
SEPTEMBER 9, 1964
POWER PLANT FIRE
SEPTEMBER 9, 1964

# Author's Note

Aleut versus Unangax

Times change and greater awareness emerges. For many years Aleutian tribal people were known as Aleuts, a name given to them by Russians in the 1700s, though they referred to themselves as Unangax. Having taken advantage of more educational opportunities and more advanced forms of communication, Native pride has become an important issue. Tribes are working to claim their true ethnic identity. Those referred to as Aleut are in transition back to what they consider their original name, Unangax. The term Aleut is still in common use, however, and was used exclusively when this story took place. To promote the chosen word, Unangax, I hope my comments and reference to this ethnic designation change will help to publicize its use.

# Cover Photograph

The cover photograph of the abandoned Dutch Harbor military base was taken in 1961 by my husband, Charlie. The scene reveals the weathered remains of what appears to be another civilization, which I guess in some ways it was. That is the backdrop for my story which begins in April, 1961.

Made in the USA
Monee, IL
28 April 2022

95589045R00089